James Logan
and the
Culture of
Provincial America

Frederick B. Tolles

James Logan
and the
Culture of
Provincial America

GREENWOOD PRESS, PUBLISHERS
WESTPORT, CONNECTICUT

Library of Congress Cataloging in Publication Data

Tolles, Frederick Barnes, 1915-
    James Logan and the culture of provincial America.

    Reprint of the ed. published by Little, Brown,
Boston, in series: The library of American biography.
    Bibliography: p.
    Includes index.
    1. Logan, James, 1674-1751. 2. Merchants--
Pennsylvania--Biography. 3. Pioneers--Pennsylvania--
Biography. 4. Pennsylvania--History--Colonial
period, ca. 1600-1775. I. Handlin, Oscar, 1915-
II. Title.
[F152.L82T64 1978]   974.8'02'0924 [B]   77-27832
ISBN 0-313-20197-8

Reprinted with the permission of Little, Brown and Company

Reprinted in 1978 by Greenwood Press, Inc.
51 Riverside Avenue, Westport, CT. 06880

Printed in the United States of America

To

Robert Glass Cleland
Godfrey Davies
French Fogle
John E. Pomfret

scholars and friends

Editor's Preface

THE FIRST AMERICANS were Europeans. Once they survived the struggle to maintain themselves in the wilderness they gave over their energies to preservation of their ties with the Old World. Yet exposure to the conditions of the New World gradually, often imperceptibly, altered them and the society in which they lived. They became new men — Americans.

Pennsylvania was among the colonies established late in the seventeenth century and its history was complicated by the Quaker strain. Nevertheless, it illustrated dramatically the general pattern in which colonial experience developed a distinctive provincial culture, neither completely autonomous nor yet completely dependent on that of the mother country.

The battle against the savage forest and the effort to penetrate into the interior created opportunities as well as problems. The course of Indian trade and diplomacy under primitive conditions called for an adaptation of skills and attitudes that came but slowly to Europeans. And even in the settled regions, a continuing succession of adjustments was necessary. Familiar English forms of political action could not readily be carried across the Atlantic. As new men asserted their own ideas and defended their own interests, they frustrated the early expectations of the Proprietor and his friends. The succession of compromises that followed recast the government of the province.

Nor could men even view themselves and their universe altogether as they had before migration. In the perspective of the New World, nature manifested itself in a variety of unexpected and unfamiliar forms. Now and again that raised troubling questions which subtly transformed every sphere of thought.

James Logan was involved in every aspect of these adjustments. A Quaker, he nevertheless was not able to accept the simple view of William Penn, the English founder of the colony. Heavily involved in the westward movement as a trader, speculator and diplomat, he became familiar with the exciting hopes and the vexatious disappointments of the frontier. As a government official, he confronted the necessities of dealing with fundamental political problems; and as a thinker and scholar, he began to make meaningful intellectual adjustments to the conditions of his environment. He was thus intimately involved with the forces that brought the culture of provincial America into being.

OSCAR HANDLIN

Contents

Editor's Preface   ix

1674 – 1699
I   A *Canterbury* Pilgrim   3

1699 – 1712
II   Proprietary Agent   15
III   "The Ministerial Part of the Government"   31
IV   Logan and the People   51
V   London and a New Beginning   76

1712 – 1726
VI   A Buffalo Skin for Dr. Fabricius   89
VII   "Preserve the Iroquois"   100
VIII   "A Wilderness of Briars and Thorns"   113

1726 – 1751
IX   Public Affairs: The Stone of Sisyphus   142
X   Logan and the Frontier   159
XI   Stenton   186
XII   Quaker Virtuoso   196

A Note on the Sources   215

Index   221

James Logan
and the
Culture of
Provincial America

I

A *Canterbury* Pilgrim

For nearly a quarter of a century they had been flocking into the Delaware Valley — Quakers fleeing from persecution and restricted opportunity in England, Wales, Ireland, the Low Countries, seeking in the New World a quiet place where they could worship God in silence and practice their callings in tranquillity. For the most part they were yeoman farmers, craftsmen, shopkeepers, men and women of little account in the lands from which they had come. But they were possessed by a burning conviction and inspired by a luminous vision. Their conviction was that God spoke directly to all men if they would only listen for His voice within them. And their vision was of nothing less than a revival of primitive Christianity, the creation of a new society in which men would live together in peace, simplicity, innocence, and love, each one responsive to the Light within him, each one sensitive to his neighbor's needs, and all bound together in a blessed community governed by the principles of the Sermon on the Mount.

In the silence of their meetings for worship they enjoyed an intimate converse with the Spirit. But in their ordinary lives they were shrewd, industrious, practical

folk, convinced that if they were to restore the primitive
Christian community, build the Kingdom of God, on
the banks of the Delaware, they must do it by working
hard in their callings, keeping to a plain way of life, making resourceful use of the materials that lay at hand. The
religious faith that inspired their prophetic vision also
instilled in them the practical virtues of diligence, frugality, prudence, and thrift. The farmer at his harvest, the
tailor with his needle, the cooper at his bench, the trades-
man in his shop — they were all, they believed, doing
God's will in the world and they could all expect, if they
were faithful, to receive His blessing in the form of material prosperity. The bright, compelling vision of a New
Testament society overspreading the Delaware Valley
might fade in time, might shrink to the narrower image of
a "peculiar people" maintaining their testimonies in quiet
isolation from their neighbors; but the ingrained habits of
industry and thrift which led to prosperity would survive
along with the spiritual way of worship and the tender
concern for human suffering.

Already, by the end of the seventeenth century, a bare
twenty-five years after the first Friends had come to the
valley, they had reason to believe that God in His providence had blessed their labors, for the broad Delaware
River flowed through a countryside smiling with prosperity, teeming with activity. The clearings between the
creeks on the level, parklike Jersey shore were punctuated
by trim brick dwellings and neat farmyards. The rolling
uplands of Bucks, Philadelphia, and Chester counties in
Pennsylvania were mantled with golden wheat fields,
dotted with substantial gray stone farmhouses. In the low-
lying "territories" of New Castle, Kent, and Sussex (which
would one day be the state of Delaware) the gold of
the wheat sometimes gave way to the bright green of
broad-leaved tobacco. There were towns along the river

too, bustling little ports, to which the Quaker farmers brought their produce and Quaker ship captains their European goods — Lewes and New Castle on the broad estuary, Salem and Burlington on the Jersey side, the thriving market town of Chester on the west bank, and, above it, Philadelphia, youngest of the river towns but already outstripping them all in size and volume of trade.

Beyond the settlements, in the back country to the west, lay a continent of untold vastness and unimagined natural wealth. Even within the bounds of William Penn's province of Pennsylvania there were endless reaches of dark, silent forest, range upon range of lofty mountains, great rivers like the Susquehanna and the upper waters of the Ohio. But this empire to the westward scarcely entered the consciousness of the Friends who dwelt in West New Jersey, Pennsylvania, and the Lower Counties. Their life was focused on the Delaware, the stream which bound them into a single community and connected them with the greater Atlantic world.

In time their valley would fill up. Settlement would reach out into the Susquehanna country and beyond. Then men would begin to look westward and sense a continental destiny. One day the westward-lookers would create an independent nation, and Philadelphia — William Penn's "green country town" at the center of the Delaware Valley — would be its first political capital. But Americans would never cease to look eastward too, would never forget that they shared a common idiom of thought with western Europe. As the American people grew to cultural maturity and assumed their place in the Atlantic community of mind and spirit, Philadelphia would be, for a time, their intellectual capital too.

James Logan came to Philadelphia in 1699, a mere secretary in the service of William Penn. During a great part of the next half century, until he died in 1751, full of years and honors, he was the region's most influential statesman, its most distinguished scholar, its most respected — though not its most beloved — citizen. He looked both westward and eastward — westward to the frontier of the Indian, the fur trader, the pioneer settler; eastward to the seat of the British mercantile empire, the traditional springs of European humanistic culture, the new sources of scientific knowledge. But he was not simply a spectator, a detached onlooker at these worlds. As businessman, politician, administrator, scholar, he took a dominating part in the life of his time and place, and, to a degree not given to many men, shaped its course. Easily the most considerable man in the Delaware Valley in his lifetime, he was, take him by and large, one of the three or four most considerable men in colonial America.

His origins were inconsiderable enough. His father was a penurious Scotch Quaker schoolmaster. A man of learning, Master of Arts from Edinburgh University, Patrick Logan had once been in holy orders, had occupied a comfortable position as chaplain to the wife of a Scottish peer at Stenton, his own native place in East Lothian. But he had listened to some traveling Quaker minister who visited Stenton, some "public Friend" who persuaded him that mere human learning was no qualification for the Gospel ministry. Troubled in spirit, "convinced" in his heart that the only true religion was an inward experience of God's presence, a direct communication of His light and love, Patrick Logan had given up his profitable chaplaincy and become one of the despised people called Quakers.

Life in seventeenth-century Scotland was grim enough for a man with no land and no powerful friends or family connections. (There seems to be no solid ground for the belief, cherished by later Logans, that Patrick was descended from the Lairds of Restalrig, and anyhow that family had been attainted of treason in James I's time.) For a Quaker in that ironbound Calvinist land, life was all but impossible. So Patrick Logan had followed several generations of Lowland Scots across the Irish Sea to Ulster. There he found a home and a position as schoolmaster at Lurgan in County Armagh, not many miles inland from Belfast.

Here, on October 20, 1674, James Logan was born. His mother, Isabel Hume, had connections with several landed families in the Lowlands, but she too had sacrificed her status by becoming a Quaker. She bore Patrick nine children, though only James and his younger brother William survived childhood.

Lurgan's Quaker meeting was the oldest in the country. It had been established twenty years earlier by the redoubtable founder of Irish Quakerism, William Edmondson, whom his fellow Friends called "the great hammer of Ireland." But Quakerism had not prospered in Lurgan, and teaching the children of a handful of impoverished and persecuted Friends provided Patrick Logan but a meager living. James Logan grew up in humble circumstances. "A weaver's trade," he would later write, "might have suited my birth." Only unceasing diligence and God's blessing, he felt, had raised him and his brother William "above the degree of laborers with the axe and spade."

Life was hard for a Quaker family of any condition in Ireland. Friends suffered constantly for their conscientious refusal to pay tithes, to swear oaths, to attend worship in the Established Church. Regularly the parish officers would descend upon the poor Lurgan Friends, enter their houses to distrain their goods, and ride off with a pewter vessel, an ax, or a pot, often worth twice or three times the amount of the tithe or fine. Sometimes there would be violence. A neighbor of the Logans, hauling a load of timber to Dundalk, was stopped one day by the lieutenant of a troop of horse. Who was he? the officer demanded — a papist, a Tory marauder? No, replied the Quaker, keeping his hat on — "an honest man." Whereupon the lieutenant beat him with his staff, kicked him, tried to ride him down with his horse. Finally he sent the unoffending Quaker on his way, calling out after him that "he might thank God that his horse had more mercy than himself, or else he would have trod out his guts."

Petty persecution of this sort was the lot of every Irish Quaker in the reign of Charles II, but in the years that followed, worse was in store. James Logan was still a pupil in his father's school when James II came to the throne in 1685. Old William Edmondson, standing in Lurgan meetinghouse, prophesied a time of "great exercises and trials approaching." The Lord, he thundered, would "spread the carcasses of men on the earth, as dung." For now, with a Catholic monarch on the throne, the Irish were up in arms. Wandering bands of Tories or "rapparees" plundered and laid waste the houses and fields of the Protestants. As Edmondson described it, "it looked like a sudden famine, there was such great destruction."

Poverty, alienation from the world about him, insecurity, fear — these were the conditions of James Logan's boyhood. "In the days which should have been my gayest," he later wrote, "I knew nothing out of school but terror and horror." Only in the classroom could James Logan feel secure and content, for Patrick Logan was a good teacher and James an apt pupil. Before he was thirteen the boy knew Latin and Greek and had made a beginning in Hebrew. But learning was of little immediate worth to a poor Quaker boy, since the professions — medicine, the law, the army, the church — were all closed to him. When he was thirteen his parents sent him up to

Dublin to be apprenticed to a Quaker merchant named Edward Webb. Webb was a linen draper, "one as considerable with his partner," James Logan later recalled, "as any in Dublin."

He served Edward Webb only six months, however, for in 1688, when James II was deposed and his army retreated to Ireland, that country felt at last the full fury of the calamity William Edmondson had foretold. James's parents summoned him home to Lurgan. It was a frightful time for Protestants in Ireland. "Now was wickedness let loose and got an head," wrote Edmondson, "so that by violence and cruelty most of our Protestant neighbors were forced from their dwellings." The army of James II, marching to besiege Londonderry, only fifty miles away, sacked the little town, and the Logans fled back across the Irish Sea to Scotland.

In the spring of 1689 the family was in Edinburgh, destitute save for the charity of local Friends. So "broken" was James Logan's constitution that, as he later wrote, he "could never bear hardships" thereafter. The following spring, Patrick Logan went to London for the Quakers' Yearly Meeting. There he met some Friends from Bristol, who invited him to become their schoolmaster. It was more than a year before the family could be reunited, but in Bristol there was at last some prospect of security. James Logan had just passed his seventeenth birthday.

Bristol in the 1690's was a booming town, the second seaport for size in England and the British Empire. Its very streets seemed bristling with masts, for the Avon and Frome rivers brought the trading ships into the heart of the city. Bristol's prosperity was founded on trade with America. Its Quaker community — forty years old now — shared fully in the trade and in the prosperity. With time and growing wealth had come respectability. Some of the leading Quakers — merchants, grocers, linen drapers — were already serving as Guardians of the Poor; within a few years they would become eligible to be Burgesses. Perhaps it was but just recompense for the persecution they had borne, but some London Quakers, less complacent, said they "feared Friends of Bristol were grown covetous."

For three years Patrick Logan taught the sons of these Quaker burghers in his schoolroom on the second floor of the Friars Meetinghouse, just outside the city walls. But he was not content there. Like many another schoolteacher, he "could not brook the mothers' taking upon them to direct his treatment of their children." So in the autumn of 1693, the troubles in Ireland being temporarily quieted, he went back to Lurgan, leaving his nineteen-year-old son in charge of the school.

While young Logan taught the rudiments of learning to the Quaker children of Bristol, he also advanced his own education. Mathematics especially fascinated him. Already, in Edinburgh, he had discovered and mastered a wonderful book by William Leybourn — his *Cursus mathematicus,* an immense folio which gathered up in nine hundred pages most of the mathematical and astronomical knowledge of the day. He cultivated languages too, perfected his Latin and Greek, made further progress in Hebrew, learned French, Italian, a smattering of Spanish. All this he accomplished by himself without teachers, except for a French master who helped him with pronunciation.

If young James Logan had an insatiable thirst for learning, he hungered also for wealth and station. He had begun to collect a library, and books cost money — more than the forty or fifty pounds a year that a Quaker schoolmaster could earn. It would have been hard in any case to avoid the contagion of trade and money-getting in Bristol. Hardly a soul in that bustling seaport but ventured something, however little, in the ships that sailed regularly for the American colonies. Even "a poor shopkeeper that sells candles," it was said, "will have a bale of stockings, or a piece of stuff for Nevis or Virginia."

James Logan could not resist the attraction of profits in trade. In 1697, the Treaty of Ryswick having made the seas safe for commerce, he resolved to close his school and settle on the island of Jamaica as an agent for some of the Bristol merchants. So successful, so popular had he been as a teacher that his pupils went home on the last day in tears — "one young thing excepted," he later recalled — and he was offered a profitable place as master of the public grammar school. But to accept that post he would have had to conform to the Church of England, and Patrick Logan's son was too much a Quaker to be tempted, even by a place worth two hundred pounds. Anyhow, the rewards of trade promised to be even greater.

He went over to Ireland to take leave of his parents. His mother, who had lost seven of her children, would not hear of his going to the West Indies: tearfully she told him she would rather see him dead. So James went instead to Dublin, to his old master Edward Webb, and offered to act as his agent in Bristol. But Webb and the other linen drapers already had their settled correspondents there. If the young man wished to enter the linen trade, it was clear he must do it on his own. Regretfully, Logan sold his only valuable assets, his library of more than seven hundred volumes, invested the receipts in a cargo of linens, and returned to Bristol. For eight months he struggled to break into the closed circle of cloth merchants with little success. Then one spring day in 1699 William Penn sent for him.

Now that George Fox, founder of the Quaker movement, was dead, Penn was the most famous Friend of the
day. People knew him as the son of an admiral, an Oxford
man and a landed gentleman, who had long ago cast in
his lot with the humble Quakers and had devoted his
great talents to propagating and defending their doctrine
of the Inward Light. They knew him as a fearless
preacher and writer who had suffered in the Tower of
London for his opinions. They knew him too in his para-
doxical role as courtier and confidant of kings. But most
of all they knew him — especially the Bristol people, who
had such close ties with America — as the founder of
Pennsylvania, the man who, having imagined an ideal
commonwealth of peace and freedom, had actually
brought it to pass in the valley of the Delaware.

Penn had not been in America for a decade and a half.
The past two years he had been living in Bristol, where he
had found and married his second wife, Hannah Callowhill, daughter of a prominent linen merchant. Logan
had seen the great man often, had heard him preach in
the Friars Meetinghouse. On occasion Penn had visited
his classroom, for he was one of the committee appointed
by Bristol Monthly Meeting to supervise the school. Evi-
dently he thought well of the young man, for he had a
proposal to make to him. He was about to go back to
Pennsylvania. Would James Logan go along as his secretary?

This time Logan did not consult his mother. He considered the invitation for several days, then rode to Bath,
where Penn was taking the waters, and accepted. When
the Proprietor of Pennsylvania with his wife Hannah and
his twenty-year-old daughter Letitia sailed from Ports-
mouth on the *Canterbury* in September, James Logan,
not yet twenty-five, accompanied them.

The crossing was tedious. It took three months and

near the end of it there were violent storms. In that three months Logan grew well acquainted with his new master and with his wife and daughter. He never forgot an incident which took place one day on shipboard. An armed vessel hove into sight and seemed about to give chase. The captain straightway cleared the *Canterbury's* decks for action. Knowing the Quakers' religious testimony against fighting, he told Penn and his party they might retire into the cabin. This they did — all except Logan, who stayed on deck and was assigned to a gun. As it turned out, there was no fighting, for the other ship proved to be friendly. When Logan went below to tell his master, Penn rebuked him before the whole company of Friends. Why, he demanded, had he stayed on deck and assisted in preparations for defense, contrary to Quaker principles? Piqued by the reproof, Logan responded bluntly: "I being thy servant, why did thee not order me to come down? But thee was willing enough that I should stay and help to fight the ship when thee thought there was danger."

So, at least, Logan told the story, years later, to Benjamin Franklin, and Franklin, later still, set it down in his *Autobiography*. It may not be accurate in detail, but there is no reason to doubt that the incident occurred. Some such incident was bound to happen sooner or later, for there was a basic temperamental difference between the two men and the difference could not but be reflected in their attitudes toward the Quaker faith and its cardinal tenet of nonresistance. William Penn was by nature an enthusiast, an idealist; to him nonresistance was an integral part of the New Testament vision of life to which he was committed. In practice, as Proprietor of a great province in the British Empire, he might sometimes have to compromise his absolute testimony, but he would always cling tenaciously to the principle. Logan, on the other hand, was a practical, earth-bound man, whose religious faith could never carry him beyond the limits of reason and experience. To him nonresistance was a noble ideal for which the world was not ready, and he felt no inner compulsion to lead the way. Under Penn's tutelage he would try sincerely to stretch his faith so as to encompass the whole Quaker vision, but he would never really succeed, and he was too honest to pretend that he did. Obviously, the Quakerism of these two men was of two different orders. Yet there existed between them the basis for a loyalty, a respect, and an affection strong enough to survive the differences and grow with the passing years.

I I

Proprietary Agent

It was late in November, 1699, when the *Canterbury*, battered and sea-worn from a wild northwester encountered off Cape Henlopen, entered Delaware Bay, and sailed up the river, bringing the Proprietor of Pennsylvania back to his province. The people, who had not seen him for fifteen years, lined the shores to bid him welcome. At Chester, an un-Quakerly salute was fired from two rusty cannon and an overzealous young man lost an arm in the resulting explosion. All Philadelphia was at the waterside on December 3 to see the Proprietor step ashore with his wife, his daughter, and his secretary.

The man they saw was a portly middle-aged gentleman, bewigged and benignant. In his face and bearing were written the strain of three months at sea and the long succession of troubles and frustrations he had suffered in England since his last visit to them. Hannah Penn, a large handsome woman, twenty-seven years younger than her husband, was obviously great with child — and this was a good omen, for an American-born heir, the people thought, would bind the Proprietary family more closely to the province. Their eyes intent on the Proprietor and his family, few Philadelphians troubled to notice the tall young man of twenty-five who attended them.

From the wharf the party passed to Deputy-Governor Markham's house for a formal visit, then, since it was the First Day of the week, to the meetinghouse, where the people gave thanks for their Proprietor's safe arrival and Penn himself preached and prayed. The town which James Logan glimpsed as they passed through the streets was a little Bristol, a booming mart of trade on the riverside — or rather, a little London, for most of its buildings were constructed in the style of the red-brick metropolis which had risen from its own ashes after the Great Fire of 1666. To a new arrival like Logan, who knew the ancient cities of Dublin, Edinburgh, and Bristol, it might seem raw, crude, insignificant. But to its inhabitants Philadelphia was a "noble and beautiful city," its houses "stately," its market place "handsome," its townhouse "noble," its shipyards, brewhouses, mills, and ropewalks "spacious and commodious." In the brief space of seventeen years it had grown from a cluster of primitive caves in the riverbank to a city of nearly a thousand buildings and five thousand souls. There was no mistaking the promise of its energy, of the bustle in its streets. Even the most sophisticated newcomer could agree with Gabriel Thomas, the town's most enthusiastic booster, that before long it would "make a fine figure in the world, and be a most celebrated emporium."

Already Philadelphia's commerce rivaled New York's. William Penn had located his capital wisely. Situated at the very heart of the fertile Delaware Valley, it drew lumber and Indian corn from West Jersey, wheat, flour, beef, and pork from the farms of Bucks and Chester, furs and skins from the dense forests to the westward, grain and tobacco from the Lower Counties. From the wharves that jutted into the river sailed Philadelphia-built brigs and snows, carrying lumber and provisions to the Caribbean and the Wine Islands, tobacco and furs direct to England. They returned to the Delaware, laden with sugar, molasses, rum, wines, textiles, and hardware, laden too with people — new settlers by the scores, indentured servants, bound to labor for a term of years before becoming freeholders themselves, an occasional "public Friend" traveling in the ministry, linking the newest Quaker community to the older ones with invisible cords of love and fellowship in a common faith.

Though most of the Philadelphians were Friends, the town was beginning to lose its austere Quaker cast. Small groups of Anglicans, Swedish Lutherans, Presbyterians, and Baptists had built churches in the town. But the three plain Quaker meetinghouses — without pulpit or altar, furnished only with rows of simple, hard benches and a "gallery" in front for the elders and "public Friends" — were still the largest houses of worship. And the town's most substantial citizens, the men who carried the greatest weight in government and basked in the Proprietor's special favor, were the rising Quaker merchants — shrewd, pious, successful businessmen, much like the Bristol burghers whose children Logan had lately been teaching in England.

Logan soon became acquainted with these men. One of them, Edward Shippen, immediately put his own house on Dock Creek at the Proprietor's disposal. In a few weeks, however, Penn with his family moved nearer the center of town into Samuel Carpenter's new mansion. Carpenter dominated the province's flour and lumber trade, owned the biggest wharf in the Delaware, and was generally accounted the richest man in Philadelphia. In this "slate-roof house" Logan came to know the other grandees of the province — Richard Hill, a bluff Quaker sea captain from Maryland; Dr. Griffith Owen, a well-loved

Welsh physician and Quaker minister; Thomas Story, an English "public Friend," trained in the law, whom Penn persuaded to settle down in Philadelphia as Master of the Rolls; Isaac Norris, a young merchant of Logan's age, recently arrived from Jamaica and already well established in trade.

Owen and Story were men of some education, though as ministers, bowing to the Quaker prejudice against a learned clergy, they were careful not to parade their scholarship. The rest were graduates of the quarterdeck or the countinghouse, their reading, save for the Bible and a few "Friends' books," confined to ledgers, logbooks, and bills of lading. At first they found Penn's stiff, erudite young secretary a trifle priggish and pedantic. "I . . . should be proud of his society," wrote Norris to his brother-in-law in England, "but discretion, I think, must forbid it, lest I (who am by barefaced profession a mere Pennsylvanian) should corrupt him."

Though Penn depended on these townsmen for political support, he was himself by birth and personal preference a country gentleman. "The world," he thought, "is apt to stick close to those who have lived and got wealth" in cities. So as soon as the ice was out of the river and Hannah Penn out of childbed (her first child, John, was born at the end of January), he moved his family to Pennsbury, his imposing country seat, twenty-seven miles up the Delaware. James Logan remained behind in Carpenter's mansion with plenty of duties to keep him busy. The Pennsbury manor house with all its outbuildings was not yet quite complete. Logan must hire carpenters, joiners, plumbers, and provide adequate quantities of ale and rum for them; he must go from warehouse to warehouse, from wharf to wharf along the Philadelphia waterfront, to buy bricks, lime, tiles, deal boards, nails, linseed oil, hardware to send up the river; he must perform a hundred trivial errands for Hannah Penn. "Must desire thee," she would write, "to send the two pair of pewter candle-sticks, some great candles . . . and a dozen pounds smaller ditto. . . . Call Betty Webb to thy assistance: let her send two mops to wash house with, four silver salts, and the two-handle porringer that is in my closet . . . and if any ship with provisions come from Rhode Island, I would have thee buy a firkin, two or three as price and worth is, of good butter, also cheese and candles, etc. for winter's store. . . ." Yet Hannah Penn was thoughtful of the secretary's welfare too. "I believe thou hast been sometimes too lonely," she wrote solicitously at the end of her long letter of requests.

Actually, he was too busy to be lonely. Penn was disabled most of the summer with a badly swollen leg and seldom came to town, even though he could make the journey in comfort and state on his splendid barge. Moreover, he did not like to be troubled with details. "Stop all business from coming hither," he wrote petulantly from Pennsbury at the end of June. Sometimes it was hard to know how to please the Proprietor. Down from Pennsbury came a peremptory command: "Prepare a nervous proclamation against vice." Logan set to work, composed a solemn, emphatic warning to all who maintained or patronized grogshops and disorderly houses, copied it out fair in a large, clear hand, and sent it up the river. Back from Pennsbury came a sharp rebuke. The Secretary had presumed too much. Penn had not meant for Logan to write a proclamation for him to sign, but merely to draft one for him to correct and submit to the Council.

The secretary's chief responsibility — the only one that made him feel he was more than a mere clerk and lackey — proved the most arduous, the most distasteful and frustrating. By the terms of his charter from King Charles II,

William Penn was absolute lord of the soil in Pennsylvania, feudal proprietor of a vast domain greater in extent than any medieval duchy or barony in England. Like the Calverts of Maryland and the proprietors of the Carolinas, Penn expected to draw an income from the sale of lands in his province. Logan was to act as his land agent — to collect for tracts already taken up but not paid for, to sell more lands, to get in the quitrents (feudal dues of a shilling or a bushel of wheat for every hundred acres) which every settler owed the Proprietor. Penn's need for money was urgent. His accustomed way of living was expensive and he had incurred heavy debts while fighting for his province at court. He had sunk nearly twenty-five thousand pounds in Pennsylvania, and had got back from land sales and quitrents barely one thousand pounds. Now he looked to his secretary to put the province on a paying basis.

Logan found Penn's American affairs in baffling confusion — no rent rolls; no accounts of money paid in or sums still owed; surveys invariably inadequate, often inaccurate, sometimes overlapping; the quitrents years overdue, and the people rebellious at the very idea of such quasi-feudal encumbrances on the soil of the New World. Logan despaired of bringing order into this stubborn chaos. At the end of eight months he was ready to give up and go back to Bristol. But Penn persuaded him to stay by promising to have the Assembly pass a law of property to regularize land transactions. The law was enacted in November 1700. It confirmed all earlier grants, even when formal patents had not been issued; it declared that all future grants should give absolute rights, except for the obligation to pay quitrents; it provided for resurveys where lines were uncertain or conflicting. Now, with firm legal ground under his feet, Logan could approach the people in the Proprietor's name with more assurance.

But still the money came in slowly. In May 1701 Penn
sent him southward on tour through Chester and New
Castle counties to inspect titles, order resurveys, issue
patents, collect quitrents. For Logan it was a welcome opportunity, after his winter's confinement in town, to see
the country at its loveliest — the woods dazzling with
white dogwood, redolent with fragrant myrtle, besprin-
kled with vivid wildflowers. But the financial returns
were disappointingly meager. He was dismayed at the
hostility of the people in New Castle County toward
Penn and the Quaker government.

The Lower Counties had been settled long before the
Quakers' coming by Swedes, Finns, Dutchmen; more recently there had been small settlements of French,
Scotch, and English immigrants. Few were Friends, and
few sympathized with Quaker pacifism in government —
the less so, perhaps, because of their vulnerable situation
at the mouth of Delaware Bay, where they lay open to attack by marauding pirates or hostile French men-of-war.
The people of the Lower Counties even questioned Penn's
right to the soil and the government. Some insisted that
Penn had never received these rights from the Duke of
York; others said the Duke had never had a valid title in
any case; still others pointed out that Lord Baltimore
claimed the region and that if they paid Penn for it they
might some day have to pay all over again. Logan came
back to Philadelphia with little to show for his efforts — a
scant ten pounds in cash and fifty pounds in wheat.

He found Penn preparing reluctantly to go back to
England. A series of alarming letters had warned him that
strenuous efforts were on foot there to nullify all proprietary charters, bring all the American provinces directly under royal control. Logan was ready to go back
to England too, but Penn prevailed on him to stay. The
Proprietor had become dependent on his efficient young

secretary. Though Logan might be discouraged at the small amount of money he had raised in two years, Penn knew it was more than he had realized from his province in the preceding seventeen.

Before sailing, Penn loaded his secretary with new offices. He made Logan Clerk of the Council, Secretary of the Province, and, along with Shippen, Dr. Owen, and Thomas Story, Commissioner of Property, responsible for all transactions involving lands. He authorized him, with Isaac Norris, to make remittances to England and officially appointed him Receiver-General for Pennsylvania, the Lower Counties, East and West Jersey, and "any other part or place of America." These offices, Logan knew, promised little in the way of honor, status, or emolument, but much in the way of labor, frustration, and unpopularity.

There was one more important responsibility which Penn chose to entrust to his young secretary. As Proprietor of Pennsylvania, Penn had a special role as suzerain and protector of its aboriginal inhabitants, the Indians who had roamed its forests for centuries before he had come. As a Quaker, he had always been concerned to keep his relations with these people on a friendly footing of mutual respect and trust. Before departing for England, he convened a council of Indians in the great hall at Pennsbury. Graciously he spoke of his affection for them, explained why he must leave them for a while, reminded them of their former agreements, expressed his wish to brighten the covenant chain which bound them together. Solemnly the Indians promised that, if differences should arise, they would not go to war, "but justice should be done in all such cases, that all animosities might be prevented on all sides forever." Then Penn pointed Logan out as "the person particularly entrusted to take care of them in his behalf." The speechmaking over, everyone went outside, where the Indians sat in a circle about the fire and sang "a melodious hymn," all the while beating on the ground with little sticks. Finally — so a curious English observer noted in his journal — "they rose up and danced a little about the fire, and parted with some shouting like triumph or rejoicing."

A few weeks later, on the deck of the *Dolmahoy,* which was to take him to England, Penn handed his secretary a detailed letter of instructions. Clearly he expected much of the young man. "Get in quitrents," he ordered; "sell lands. . . . Get in the taxes . . . and use thy utmost diligence in making remittances to me. . . . Pay off all my notes and orders on thee, settle my accounts, discharge all my debts honorably but carefully, make rent rolls. . . . Get my two mills finished. . . . Cause all the province and territories to be resurveyed. . . . Write to me diligently, advising me of everything relating to my interest." It was a heavy responsibility for an ex-schoolmaster who, until recently, had been more concerned with gerunds and hexameters than with tax lists and land surveys, more familiar with Greek heroes and Roman orators than with frontier farmers and Indian sachems.

James Logan was no longer simply a clerk, standing obscurely in the Proprietor's shadow; he was now William Penn's chief American representative in business affairs. His master's demands for money, he soon found, were insistent. "Hasten over rents, and all thou canst," Penn wrote from England, soon after landing, "for many call upon me for old scores, thinking I have brought over all the world with me." At first, Logan was full of assurance, confident that he could meet all the Proprietor's needs. He estimated that he could easily collect twenty-one thousand seven hundred pounds, Pennsylvania currency, within three years, the bulk of it from land sales. With these receipts he would buy bills of exchange — negotiable drafts on London merchants — and thereby convert Pennsylvania assets into sterling credits for the Proprietor.

His self-confidence did not outlast the winter. The prosperity which had pervaded the Delaware Valley when he first arrived suddenly ended in 1702 as rumors of war reached the colony — war between France and Britain over the succession to the Spanish throne. French corsairs, preying on the West Indies trade, soon ruined the market for Pennsylvania provisions and cut off the vital flow of gold and silver from the Spanish islands. Without Spanish dollars, Logan found, he could not buy bills of exchange. Privateers, hovering off the Capes, menaced shipments of tobacco from the Lower Counties, and cut off the only means of making direct returns to England. Even when the ships got through, Delaware tobacco brought a poor price; Logan found it "the greatest cheat as well as slavery in trade."

Province and territories slumped into depression. In Chester County, where the thrifty, loyal Quaker farmers were willing to pay their quitrents but unable to secure any hard cash, Logan was often forced to accept wheat. But wheat that brought no price, that was merely a dead weight on the collector's hands, did William Penn in England no good. By May 1702 Logan had to report dolefully that he had collected barely twelve pounds in quitrents and less than fifty pounds from the sale of lands. Much of what he did raise he had to pay out on the spot to satisfy Penn's local creditors. When his collections exceeded Penn's oustanding debts, it was a puzzle to know how to make remittances, especially after the "cruisers of Martinico" ruined the provision trade.

But Logan had a good stock of ingenuity and native

business acumen. Driven willy-nilly into the intricate, risky channels of trade, Logan found he could invest Penn's money in Pennsylvania wheat, flour, or beer, send them in one of Norris's or Shippen's vessels to South Carolina to be traded for rice, to Central America for logwood, to Newfoundland for codfish, to Madeira for wine, or to the nearby Chesapeake colonies for bills of exchange. Ultimately the profits from these transactions — if the ships escaped the prowling privateers — would find their way into Penn's hands.

Furs and skins always found a ready market in England. "Oh that we had a fur-trade instead of a tobacco one," wrote Penn at the end of 1702, "and that thou wouldst do all that is possible to master furs and skins for me, but bears more especially." In a moment of wild fantasy Penn even proposed that Logan secure for him a monopoly of the fur trade. The young secretary soon brought him to his senses. To expect Pennsylvanians to grant a monopoly, he wrote, was "as vain as to expect they will make offerings of their whole estates to thee." Obviously Penn did not understand the New World. There was no place there for special, exclusive privileges. But "contrivance and management," Logan believed, would give Penn a reasonable share in the trade. By "contrivance and management" Logan presently became as skillful as any Philadelphia merchant in dealing with Indians and backwoods traders as well as with the experienced businessmen of Front Street.

He was grossly underpaid, for Penn had been characteristically casual about financial arrangements. He received a small stipend for copying laws and keeping the Council's minutes; he could collect fees for making out land warrants and patents; he was entitled to a commission of five per cent on the quitrents he gathered. But these fees and commissions all together came to barely one hundred pounds, too little for a bachelor to subsist on in comfort, far too little for a man who yearned to live well, to buy books, to marry and raise a family. He often complained to Penn that he got nothing for his ingenuity and pains in finding ways to make remittances. "Returns are my care," he sighed, "and if they yield me nothing proportionable to my trouble, I lose the bloom of my youth in vain, and in time to come shall make my decayed strength a monument of folly to instruct those that come after to beware."

Unprofitable though it was to him, trade was at least exciting compared with the dull chore of collecting quitrents. "It would keep a man and a horse employed," he grumbled, "only to go a-dunning." Selling lands was even more tedious. The four Commissioners of Property sat regularly once or twice a week at the "slate-roof house" to issue warrants for surveys, set prices, grant patents, settle disputes. Logan, as secretary, was saddled with most of the work, for Shippen, he soon found, was "too thronged in his own affairs," and Owen and Story were too unworldly for such mundane business. It was thankless labor, managing Penn's land office. "I am left exposed," he complained, considered "severe and cruel by exacting of prices which yet I know are still too moderate and low . . . universally found fault with by the common vogue of the country."

His predicament became all the more intolerable when the Proprietor's political enemies, quick to scent oppression, made issues of his quitrent and land policies. The charter of Pennsylvania had given William Penn both ownership of the soil and responsibility for administration; he was both Proprietor and Governor. The charter had further stipulated that he must govern with the advice and approbation of the freemen of the province; and indeed Penn, a Whig by political conviction, was committed to the principle of representative government. Yet theory and practice — the doctrines of the radical Whig and the interests of the feudal Proprietor — sometimes conflicted. Logan was bothered by no theoretical commitment to popular rule. His temperament, his political philosophy, and the nature of his duties all tended to align him on the side of Proprietary prerogative, made him an object of suspicion and distrust to those in the provincial Assembly and out of it who were disaffected toward the Proprietor, and who, from principle or self-interest, exalted the privileges of the people.

Personal loyalty to Penn, a strong sense of the obligation of contracts, his temperamental bias toward prerogative rule all drove him to exact every penny to which his master was entitled. Yet the scarcity of coin in the colony was obvious, and when he resorted to distraint proceedings and seized the goods of the delinquents, he sometimes found that these extreme measures produced no money, only ill will. One cantankerous Philadelphia merchant, Joshua Carpenter, stoutly refused to pay his quitrents, and threatened the undersheriff, who tried to collect them, with prosecution. Determined to outwit the Proprietary authorities, he concealed all his plate, his pewter, his other distrainable goods, and lived for two months in a bare house, "drinking out of nothing but earthenware." Finally Logan attached his house, a fine mansion on Chestnut Street. Carpenter promptly went to court and recovered his property. Worse, he gave it out that the government did not dare to keep it, "which," Logan noted sadly, "instead of forwarding the business, retards it," for every libel against the Proprietary was "greedily received by them that would have it so."

Logan's zeal in his master's behalf presently brought him under the displeasure even of his fellow Friends. Hearing that a squatter from New Jersey had settled on

one of the small reed-covered islands in the Delaware opposite Philadelphia, he rowed out one day in the summer of
1702 with the Sheriff of Philadelphia and an armed
posse to drive him off. Reports of the incident reached
the ears of Friends. They promptly called him before the
Monthly Meeting, required him to acknowledge his error
in "going with armed men . . . when he ought to have
gone in a peaceable manner, according to the profession
he makes." Logan submitted to discipline with bad grace.
He was by no means convinced that mundane affairs
could be managed without the use of force. Nevertheless,
he knew his master's views on the subject and he dutifully made his acknowledgment, praying "that it may
please God . . . so to enlighten my understanding by
His spirit that I may avoid not only all such occasions but
all others that by being contrary to His divine will may
minister offence for the future."

As if the stubborn resistance of the Pennsylvanians and
the continuing vicissitudes of wartime commerce were
not enough to dishearten the most sanguine Proprietary
agent, the summer of 1705 brought crushing news: William Penn, through his own incredible naïveté and care-
lessness, had lost control of his province. For years, Logan
knew, Penn had left the management of his business affairs in England to a Bristol Quaker, Philip Ford. What
Logan did not know was that by a systematic, long-con-
tinued course of financial jugglery, Ford had involved
his guileless master inextricably in debt to him. In 1699,
just when Logan had entered Penn's service, Ford had
engineered his final masterpiece of chicane: he had
tricked the Proprietor into confirming a document which
Penn had naïvely supposed to be a mortgage, but which
was actually a bill of sale, for the province of Pennsylvania! For six years, unbeknownst to Logan, Penn had been

renting the province from his own steward. The elder
Ford was now dead, but his widow and son were insisting
on the letter of the fraudulent bargain, and young Ford
was even reported on his way to Pennsylvania to claim
the province as his property.

Logan was dumfounded. He could understand how
Penn, pressed for funds, might have borrowed money
with the province as security, "but the granting it away
in fee without any defeasance but a lease," he wrote in
amazement, "is, if true, what none can understand." Unhappily, it was too true, and succeeding months brought
still worse news. A Chancery decision not only confirmed
the Fords' title but awarded them a large sum for arrears
of rent. Since Penn could not pay, they proceeded to have
him committed to debtors' prison. Though Logan did not
cease to scold his master for his simplicity, his gullibility,
he could not but be touched by Penn's plight.

In the circumstances there was only one thing to do:
somehow he must find ways and means to redeem the
province, rescue its rightful Proprietor from the Fords'
rapacious clutches. In six years by unceasing labor he
had managed to scrape together perhaps eight thousand
pounds from land sales and quitrents. Now, to satisfy the
Fords' usurious demands, he calculated that he would
have to raise at least thirty thousand pounds, Pennsylvania money. But with the Fords in legal possession of the
land and with all the Proprietor's enemies in Pennsylvania rejoicing in his troubles, it was impossible to collect
a penny.

Presently, however, matters began to improve. The
Fords finally overreached themselves in 1708 when they
applied to the Queen for letters patent granting them William Penn's powers of government as well as his land.
The Lord Chancellor denounced their pretensions and
opened the door for Penn to recover title to his province

if he could raise the money. The Fords now agreed to a compromise. A group of wealthy English Friends, including Thomas Callowhill, Hannah Penn's father, paid them off (at about half their original demands) and accepted a mortgage on the province as security — a solution Logan himself had proposed two years earlier.

Now as soon as Logan could obtain proper authority from the trustees under the mortgage (which would require a trip to England), he could begin to remit money to his master again. A brisk war-born trade in wheat with Portugal promised to provide the means of obtaining credit in Europe. By the end of 1709 there was at last some prospect that he might eventually be able to put William Penn's province on a paying basis. For ten years he had labored against formidable odds — the almost universal resistance of a people who instinctively found a feudal proprietorship out of place in a New World setting, the vexing problems of finding money in a colonial economy or even exportable products with which to establish credits in Europe, the exasperating, almost childlike simplicity of the aristocratic Quaker who was his master. Yet Logan's industry, his ingenuity, his imperviousness to criticism, above all his steadfast loyalty to William Penn had made him, in the teeth of the contradictions and difficulties of his position, a remarkably successful proprietary agent.

I I I

"The Ministerial Part
of the Government"

WHILE WILLIAM PENN was in his province, he exercised his powers as Governor directly. When he left for England in 1701 to defend his charter, he appointed a deputy governor, Andrew Hamilton, a capable Scotchman, who was already serving as Governor of East and West Jersey. At the same time, he made James Logan Clerk of the Council and Secretary of the Province. Of themselves these offices carried little political weight. But Penn, impressed by the young man's energy and loyalty, clearly expected him to play a role in provincial politics. In his parting letter of instructions, he spoke feelingly of the need to "soften angry spirits and . . . reduce them to a sense of their duty." Logan knew well enough who the "angry spirits" were. As soon as he was back in Philadelphia after seeing the Proprietor off in the *Dolmahoy*, he arranged "a small treat" at Andrew's tavern for Governor Hamilton and the leading malcontents. The love feast, he reported confidently to Penn, was "very well timed and managed"; there was every reason to believe it would be "of good service."

The principal guest, besides the Governor, was John Moore, Advocate of the Vice-Admiralty Court. He and

Colonel Robert Quary, the Vice-Admiralty Judge and Surveyor of Customs, were the chief representatives of royal authority in the Delaware Valley. Between these agents of the King and the freedom-loving people of Pennsylvania a kind of nonviolent guerrilla warfare had developed and the Proprietary authorities found themselves harried from both sides. Only five years before, in 1696, Parliament had moved to tighten up the lax enforcement of the Acts of Trade and Navigation, to bring some measure of order into the administration of the empire. It had passed an act setting up Admiralty courts in the colonies, requiring that every proprietary governor receive the royal approbation before taking office and give bond for the faithful execution of the acts relating to trade. The act of 1696 was a clear infringement upon colonial charters, and nowhere had resistance been stiffer than in Pennsylvania. The new Admiralty courts, empowered to seize property at wharfside and condemn it without jury trial, seemed to be taking away the protection of the common law. The Pennsylvanians felt outraged. After all, they had told Penn, "they came hither to have more and not less freedom than at home."

The people found an effective voice for their discontent in David Lloyd, a fiery Welsh Quaker, who had been Attorney-General of the province. Lloyd was unquestionably an able lawyer, though Logan found him "a man very stiff in all his undertakings . . . extremely pertinacious, and somewhat revengeful." Lloyd had made himself a popular hero by a bit of courtroom dramatics. When the Admiralty court had seized a cargo of European goods in the Delaware for noncompliance with the customs regulations, he had calmly advised the local magistrate to defy the royal authority by removing the goods from the King's warehouse at New Castle — by force, if necessary. This was not all. He had openly and flagrantly committed lese majesty by picking up the royal marshal's commission, pointing to the King's image on the seal, and remarking contemptuously: "Here is a fine baby, a pretty baby, but we are not to be frightened with babies." Indeed, he had compounded the offense — so it was said — by insisting that those who acknowledged the court's authority were "greater enemies to the liberties and properties of the people than those that set up ship money in King Charles I's time."

As representatives of the Proprietor, Logan and Hamilton found themselves awkwardly in the middle of this conflict, caught in an unrelenting crossfire. "Some of the most noted Friends," Logan observed, "were involved or concerned more or less in David's business, and though troubled at his stiffness, yet wished him in the right because [he was] the most active enemy . . . against the other party, who on all occasions would be glad, they thought, of their utter ruin." The "other party" — Moore, Quary, the Crown officials — were determined to see the royal authority acknowledged in Pennsylvania. If the local resistance continued, the upshot might be nothing less than the voiding of the Proprietary charter, the loss of all the special rights and privileges enjoyed by the Quakers, the end of Penn's "holy experiment." Indeed, Colonel Quary was at this very moment in London, pressing charges against Pennsylvania before the Board of Trade and Plantations, the principal body in England concerned with colonial affairs.

The situation, Logan knew, was serious. Quary had powerful friends in England — men like Edward Randolph, Surveyor-General of the Customs, and William Blathwayt, one of the Commissioners of Trade and Plantations. These men were sworn enemies of all proprietary charters, bent on bringing all overseas colonies under direct royal control. Quary was playing their game by feeding them sheaves of petitions, complaints, affidavits, documents taxing the Proprietary government of Pennsylvania with all manner of crimes, inefficiencies, irregularities. A certain Quaker jury, read one complaint, had reached its decision by flipping a coin. The other charges were equally outrageous. William Penn, fighting desperately for his charter and the precious liberties of his people, found himself continually caught off balance by Quary's "swish-swash bounces." He denied the most flagrant misrepresentations and countered with charges that Quary was willfully untruthful, culpably ignorant of the law he was required to enforce, personally interested in the trade he was to regulate. Week after week, he sent off urgent requests to Logan for counteraffidavits to disprove Quary's mischievous allegations.

These Logan was usually able to secure and dispatch to England. But meanwhile Quary's satellites in Pennsylvania — especially John Moore, "that composition of wormwood and vinegar," as Logan now began to call him — would have sent over new ammunition for Quary to explode in England. There was really no limit, Logan felt, to their malice or their ingenuity. Their "sedulity to serve a dishonest cause," he sputtered, "keeps their thought constantly on the tenters, and dresses up each trivial passage in their secret cabals into a monstrous shape of malfeasance, the real subject of which is so slight where acted that the persons concerned in it scarce ever think of it more till they hear it roar from some mighty court or committee there."

Quary's friends did their best to keep the province in a turmoil so as to prove their contention that Penn and the Quakers were unfit to rule. They made the most of the fact that Governor Hamilton's commission lacked the royal approbation required under the Act of 1696, and were delighted when David Lloyd, who had his own animus against the Proprietary government, came unexpectedly to their support with the pronouncement that Hamilton was "no more than a conservator of the peace, and no governor till approved." They even injected religious issues into politics, trumping up the ingenious charge that the Quakers were oppressing their Anglican consciences. Because Quaker judges had religious scruples against taking or administering oaths, they raised the cry that justice could not be served in Pennsylvania. True, a law of 1700 specifically permitted Friends to substitute a simple affirmation for the judicial oath, but Churchmen could argue that a mere affirmation was insufficient to elicit the truth — even from themselves. A shrewd criminal before a Quaker court could bring proceedings to a standstill by simply demanding to be sworn.

Then there was the issue of defense. Quakers were well known to be conscientiously opposed to all war, all military preparations. On the other hand, Governor Hamilton was no Quaker — and that was one reason why Penn had appointed him. When news of war with France arrived, he did his best to raise a company of militia, sending drummers through the town and pouring out gallons of rum for recruiting purposes. But young Quakers, faithful to their peace testimony, could not, and young Anglicans, carefully coached by their elders, would not enlist. Bitterly Logan observed that the "hot Church party" had deliberately obstructed the recruiting "because they would have nothing done that may look with a good countenance at home."

To Logan, who could not quite bring himself to accept Quaker pacifism, it seemed criminally irresponsible to play politics with defense. He was worried over the military security not only of the Quaker provinces but of the entire British Empire in America. In May 1702 he read in a London magazine that the French in Canada had made a treaty with the Iroquois, the five powerful Indian nations whose domain stretched across western New York from the Hudson River to Lake Erie and who exercised suzerainty over the tribes in the Pennsylvania backwoods. He recognized at once what ominous news this was. He had studied the map of North America; he saw how New York's outpost, the fur-trading station of Albany, lay open to attack, how the safety of all the colonies depended on preserving "that barrier of the Five Nations." Reading the news from Montreal, he perceived the peril that few Americans comprehended and put it succinctly to Penn: "if we lose the Iroquois, we are gone by land." This, Logan knew, was not the kind of advice Penn expected from him. "Perhaps I may be thought to meddle too far," he added apologetically, "but I am sure it is worth thine and perhaps all the kingdom's consideration."

Actually, Logan was forced to "meddle" more and more in affairs of government. Governor Hamilton was capable enough; people found him an "affable, moderate man" and — surprisingly for a provincial governor — free from avarice. But he lived with his family at Perth Amboy in East Jersey and came to Pennsylvania only when official duties required his presence. He made Logan a temporary member of his Council and shifted "the whole weight of the ministerial part of the government" to his shoulders. Penn was pleased with the Secretary's aptitude for administration and only wished he were a better Quaker. "I know thy ability, doubt not thy integrity," he wrote. "I desire thy application and health, and above all thy growth in the feeling of the power of Truth; for that fits and helps us above all other things, even in business of this world, clearing our heads, quickening our spirits, and giving us faith and courage to perform."

Logan had need of a clear head and all his powers of application in the early months of 1703. For Colonel

Quary came back to Philadelphia filled with a new offi-
ciousness and arrogance after his sojourn among the great
men in London. "He appears very big upon it," Logan
reported, "struts extremely among his own herd; magni-
fies his own service and the great deference paid him."
The Colonel entertained his intimates at the coffeehouse
by describing his triumphs over Penn before the Lords of
Trade, even before the Queen herself, "at which," wrote
Logan scornfully, "that envious crew hug themselves, and
are overgrown with expectation of all becoming Dons,
etc." He devised ingenious new methods to "aggrandize"
himself, to attract public attention. An express would
clatter up to the coffeehouse: a letter for the Colonel from
Governor Nicholson of Virginia. Dramatically, Quary
would open it, read it out in a loud voice to the hangers-
on, and enjoy the sense of importance that came from being an officer of the Crown. He lost no opportunity to remind Logan that Governor Hamilton still lacked the royal
approbation.

When spring came and the ice in the Delaware broke
up, Logan had a moment of relief and rejoicing: a ship
arrived, bringing at last the document that confirmed the
Governor's authority. But the sense of triumph was brief.
At Amboy Hamilton lay seriously ill with a "putrid
and hectic fever." Near the end of April, 1703, word
came that he was dead. Logan posted across the Jerseys,
arriving at Amboy just in time "to meet the corpse at the
grave." "So . . . now," he wrote Penn dejectedly, "all
thy late pains for an approbation . . . are lost, and our
enemies unhappily gratified once more."

Until a new governor could be commissioned, the executive function devolved on the Council — a body composed almost wholly of Friends. Logan had a low opinion
of the Council's competence to govern. Its president and

titular head of the province was Edward Shippen, and Shippen, though a man of vast physical bulk, was a weak reed in government — a businessman preoccupied with his own business and a strict Quaker whose "niceness in some things," Logan feared, "will scarce suit the exigencies of our affairs."

Nevertheless Logan, mindful of Penn's hope that he would grow "in the power of Truth," and sobered by his recent disciplining at the hands of the meeting in the affair of the squatter, made an honest effort to be a more "consistent" Friend himself. But it was not easy, surrounded as he was by "angry spirits" intent on nullifying the Proprietary authority which he was laboring almost singlehanded to uphold. Often he gave way to fits of melancholy, and in his despair concluded that the "holy experiment" was foredoomed to failure and might as well be abandoned.

Colonel Quary had found a new ally in Lord Cornbury, Governor of New York and the most exalted personage in America — but withal a drunkard, a spendthrift, a sexual pervert, a grafter, and a vain fool. Cornbury came to Philadelphia to visit him in August 1703. The Colonel's faction, elated by the accession of so powerful a supporter, was riding high. One of them publicly boasted that they had "laid the government on its back and left it sprawling, unable to move hand or foot." It was clear to Logan that Quary and Cornbury were hatching a plot to have Pennsylvania and the territories annexed to New York and the Jerseys in one great dominion, over which Cornbury would preside grandly as viceroy with Quary his chief lieutenant. There was real danger that the plot might succeed, for Cornbury brought word that Penn, pushed to the wall by his creditors, was about to make terms with the Crown to surrender the government for ten thousand pounds sterling.

Logan found himself in an intolerable dilemma. He was quite prepared, after less than four years' experience in Pennsylvania, to see Penn give up his right to the government for a consideration, so long as he kept his title to the soil. Yet he could not bear to think of the government's being in the hands of a pair like Cornbury and Quary. "The thought of having rascals and such birds of prey set over us," he wrote Penn, "would congeal any honest man's blood." On the other hand, so long as the war with France continued, Quaker government was a dangerous anomaly. The horrors of Indian warfare were unquestionably coming nearer. The French were stirring up the Western Indians, even sending their spies into Pennsylvania. From the East came reports of actual attacks on the remote, unprotected seacoast villages of Wells, Cape Porpoise, and Falmouth in Maine.

In this situation it was hard to be at once a responsible public official and a consistent Friend — though Logan made a sincere attempt. When, at John Moore's dinner table, in the presence of Lord Cornbury, he heard the Quaker government criticized for its failure to take defensive measures, he spoke up stoutly for the religious principles of the Friends. "I pleaded," he wrote Penn, "that we were a peaceable people, had wholly renounced war, and the spirit of it; that we were willing to commit ourselves to the protection of God alone . . . and that those who will not [use] the sword, but by an entire resignation commit themselves to His all-powerful providence, shall never need it, but be safe under a more sure defence than any worldly arm."

It was good Quaker doctrine and, he added, "I really spoke my sentiments." Yet in another portion of his divided mind he knew that religious pacifism would not "answer in English government, nor the methods of this reign." Full of misgivings, forebodings, anxieties over the future, he poured out his troubled thoughts to William Penn. "Almighty Providence seems to be preparing the most dreadful scenes throughout the universe." Valiantly he sought to express a calm Quaker faith. "The most secure may find their enemies, and the most naked be protected." But his melancholy engulfed him and he dreaded the worst. "The whole earth, I believe, at least what is miscalled the Christian world, must undergo a universal visitation and be shaken together like brittle potsherds."

Relief came unexpectedly in the dead of winter — relief from governmental impotence, from the galling arrogance of royal officials, the overhanging threat of royal control. But with the welcome relief came new burdens and vexations for James Logan. Hitherto his task had been chiefly to defend the Proprietary government against incursions of royal authority; now he would have to defend it against itself — against the imprudence and irresponsibility of the representative whom Penn sent over to uphold his authority. It was late at night on February 2, 1703/4,* as Colonel Quary and Judge Moore were sitting in a Philadelphia tavern, drinking to the imminent downfall of the Quaker regime in Pennsylvania, that a new governor arrived, bearing a commission from William Penn with the approbation of Queen Anne. With him came the Proprietor's eldest son and heir, William Penn, Jr.

John Evans, the new governor, was barely twenty-six, three years younger than Logan himself. He was a

* In England and the colonies, where the Julian, or Old Style, calendar was in use until 1752, the New Year was considered to begin on March 25. Countries which had adopted the Gregorian, or New Style, calendar began the year on January 1, as we do. During Logan's lifetime Englishmen customarily used double dates for the period between January 1 and March 25.

Welshman, the son of one of Penn's oldest friends, and Penn was sure Logan would find him discreet and "advisable." On the other hand, being an Anglican and a man of the world, he would not be troubled by inconvenient scruples about oaths or military measures. Before sending him off to Pennsylvania, Penn had counseled the new governor to rely heavily on the Secretary's judgment and experience. For Logan, he had told him, "knows the factions, the friendly, the sincere, the hollow, the bold, the timid, the able, and the weak; whom to countenance, whom to beware of and whom to gain and use but not trust without good reason." One of Evans's first official acts was to give Logan a permanent seat on the Council.

By sending over a non-Quaker governor, duly commissioned and approved, William Penn had effectually spiked most of Colonel Quary's guns. He had been careful, in his instructions to Evans, to take particular note of the most persistent charge against the Proprietary government. "That nothing may lie at my door in reference to the defense of the country," he had written, the new governor was specifically authorized to raise a militia from among those conscientiously able to serve. Moreover, Logan's affidavits had caused the Commissioners of Trade finally to see Quary's "busy and turbulent proceedings" in a proper light, with the result that they were on the point of administering a sharp reprimand. For himself Quary now acted the part of a chastened man, entertained the new governor at dinner, and appeared "inclinable to have all old things done away."

If the coming of the Proprietor's deputy relieved Logan of some of his more onerous public responsibilities, the arrival of the Proprietor's son brought new and awkward private ones. Young William was only a year or so older than Governor Evans. His father, on his return from

America in 1701, had found him a spoiled young gallant, the boon companion of London rakehells and tavern roisterers, over his ears in debt. Shocked and saddened, Penn had agreed to pay off the debts if young William would exile himself for a while among the sober, godly Friends of Pennsylvania, there to repent of his follies and learn what it meant to be heir apparent to a great province, responsible for carrying on a "holy experiment" in government. Young William, badgered by his duns, had no choice but to go, leaving his wife and children behind. The anxious father gave Logan special instructions: "Be as much as possible in his company . . ." he begged, "and suffer him not to be in any public house after the allowed hours." The boy had wit, and it would take great wisdom to manage him. Logan must "watch him, outwit him, and honestly overreach him for his own good." Somehow he must contrive to "weigh down his levities . . . temper his resentments, and inform his understanding, since all depends upon it, as well for his future happiness as, in measure, your poor country's." It was a heavy responsibility for a mere secretary, scarcely older than his ward, but Logan dutifully accepted it. At the elder Penn's suggestion, he sent the young man to Pennsbury to spend his first days in America in a healthful outdoor life, hunting and fishing along the Delaware.

But young Penn quickly tired of the rustic isolation of Pennsbury, and came to town, hungry for companionship. For a while he boarded with Logan at Isaac Norris's house, but presently the two young men rented Clarke Hall, a large brick house on Chestnut Street, where they set up bachelors' quarters with a steward and a maid to keep house for them. Soon Governor Evans moved in with them and from time to time other young bachelors joined the ménage. For a while they enjoyed the company

of Roger Mompesson, a brilliant, heavy-drinking young
barrister, a former M.P. for Southampton, who had fled to
Pennsylvania to escape his creditors. Sometimes Harry
Brooke, another exile, the brilliant younger son of an
English baronet, came up from Lewes, where he was
wasting his literary talents in the post of Customs Collector. In this congenial circle of young blades, all nearly of
an age, all bored with the dullness of Quaker Philadelphia, Logan could relax, and enjoy for once the taste of
good talk and good living.

Their valiant effort to emulate the coffeehouse society of
Augustan London, to create an oasis of gay sophistica-
tion in the midst of Quaker Philadelphia, did not last
long. William Penn, Jr., presently went back to England
under circumstances to be described later. Mompesson
went on to New York to become Chief Justice of that
province. And Evans finally moved out in a huff when
Logan politely suggested that he bear a share of the
household expenses.

Evans's departure from Clarke Hall early in 1706
marked more than the close of a pleasant interlude. It
symbolized the end of his tutelage, the beginning of independence. What started as a petulant rejection of Logan's counsel ended as a thoroughgoing defiance of the
Proprietor, whose agent he was supposed to be. Though
Evans's rebellion exposed principally his own immatur-
ity, it reflected one of the tensions ever present in colonial
government, a tension that came into the open as often in
the royal colonies as in the proprietorships. The governor
in either case was the appointed agent of a distant source
of power. As chief executive of the colony his duty was
to exercise his derived power in the interests of his principal. But power is a heady thing, and when the source of
power is three thousand miles away, it is easy to forget

one's subordination or misconstrue one's duty. Logan, whose loyalty to the Proprietor was unshakable, could only watch John Evans's puerile rebellion with amazement and a sinking heart.

On May 14, 1706, an express galloped into the quiet Quaker town with a letter for Evans from Governor Seymour of Maryland. A French fleet was off the coast! Logan, who knew that Evans was impatient to put the province in a posture of defense, smelled a rat at once. "Smilingly" he took the Governor aside, and tasked him with having written the letter himself. Indignantly Evans denied it. He called the Council together and, with the assent of the non-Quaker members, issued a proclamation summoning the province to arms. Next day, another letter arrived with a similar warning, this one ostensibly from East Jersey. Early on the morning of the sixteenth, John French, the Sheriff of New Castle County, dashed into town, breathless, his horse exhausted and flecked with foam, to announce six French ships actually in the river, the port of Lewes already in ruins from their bombardment.

Panic and confusion seized the town. In terror some families flung their plate and other valuables into wells and privies, took to boats, and fled up the river till the creeks above Philadelphia were crowded with small craft of every kind. Women miscarried. The annual fair, just getting under way, was thrown into disorder, and all business disrupted. Meanwhile the Governor dashed about the streets, brandishing his sword, urging all men and boys to take up their arms and muster on Society Hill. Only the Quakers remained calm. It was Fifth Day, time for their midweek meeting for worship. When the hour arrived, though it was precisely when the tide was expected to bring the French ships up to the town, the meeting was held in its accustomed quiet.

From the beginning Logan had been sure that the whole affair was an outrageous fraud, a piece of amateur dramatics staged for a transparent political purpose. He quickly proposed a plan to save Evans from the effects of his own folly. He suggested that they go downstream together in a small boat; if they saw no ships, the Governor should wave a handkerchief, thus allaying the panic and removing from himself the suspicion of having created it in the first place; if, on the other hand, they should see ships coming upriver, he could return to direct the town's defense. Evans's refusal confirmed Logan's suspicions. Thereupon he himself went down the river until he met a shallop coming up, which reported seeing no hostile vessels. So, as a provincial poet later put it:

> The ev'ning did the plot's design betray;
> The farce was ended with the closing day.

All the Quakers, even faithful friends of the Proprietor like Samuel Carpenter, turned against the Governor in disgust. Their revulsion was complete when it became common gossip that he was keeping a mistress in an old log house on the edge of town, that on a recent official visit to Conestoga he had spent his time debauching the Indian women. Between Logan and Evans the former relationship of friendship and mutual confidence was irrecoverably gone. When their official duties brought them together, Logan treated the Governor with studied correctness. After all, they were William Penn's principal representatives in Pennsylvania, and an open breach between them would do the Proprietor's cause no good. But Evans's headstrong behavior, his deliberate flouting of the Quaker community, his alienation of the Proprietor's best friends, soon made it impossible to keep up even the pretense of harmony.

Early in November 1706 Logan received a disturbing

letter from the Governor, who had gone down to the
Lower Counties to open their Assembly. That body, restive under the Quaker Proprietorship, determined to
defend the Delaware against French marauders, had resolved to build a fort at New Castle, where the river nar-
rowed. To pay for it, Evans reported, they proposed to
levy a "powder tax" on every ship that entered the river:
half a pound of powder per ton for vessels of foreign
registry, a quarter pound for those whose home port was
on the Delaware. Logan promptly passed the word to
Samuel Carpenter and Richard Hill. As Quakers, as merchants, as Philadelphians, they were incensed. By what
right, they sputtered, did the Lower Counties presume to
lay a tax, a war tax at that, on Philadelphia shipping?
Though winter was setting in and travel was difficult, the
three men set off at once for New Castle to stop the mischief.

On the way, they met Evans, returning to Philadelphia.
When they remonstrated with him about the new law,
they found him cool, evasive, almost rude. Why hadn't
they told him, he asked blandly, that they objected to
having their ships taxed? Rebuffed and annoyed, the
three men turned back to Philadelphia. They foresaw
trouble, whether the bill became law or not. If it passed,
the result, Logan knew, would be "a perfect war between
Philadelphia and New Castle." If the Governor could
somehow be persuaded to withhold his signature, the
Lower Counties would surely complain to the Lords of
Trade that they were forbidden to defend themselves,
would request to be taken directly under royal rule.

Later, Logan went down to New Castle for a conference with the Assembly. Stoutly he insisted that the Pennsylvanians had by royal grant the right to free and un-
impeded navigation of the Delaware, that they could be
taxed only by their own consent or by act of Parliament.

In the end, the law was modified: Philadelphia-owned ships were excused from the tax, were required merely to call at New Castle and show their registry. But Logan knew the Philadelphia merchants would bristle at even this inconvenience, would see it as an infringement of their rights. "This town," he wrote Penn, "will sooner have their vessels fired at than obey."

He was right. The fort was completed by spring and Evans ordered the New Castle port authorities to start collecting the "powder tax." The "war" which Logan had prophesied broke out on May 1, 1707. Logan's friend Richard Hill, retired Quaker sea captain and fellow member of the Council, took command. He had a fine new sloop, the *Philadelphia,* just off the stocks and laden with provisions and lumber for Barbados. Hill gave the Governor fair warning: as a Philadelphian, he declared, he would never acknowledge the right of New Castle to interfere with the passage of his ships up and down the Delaware. Hotly the Governor replied that his fort would fire on any ship that failed to stop. While Evans galloped off to New Castle to set a watch lest Hill's ship slip by in the night, Hill stepped on the *Philadelphia's* quarterdeck and weighed anchor in broad daylight.

A mile above New Castle, a customs officer came aboard, demanded to see the ship's register. Hill refused. The customs officer departed, and Hill boldly sailed his sloop under the guns of the fort. Governor Evans ordered two cannon fired: one ball passed directly over the ship. Evans then set out in pursuit in a small boat. Hill put over to Salem on the Jersey side, where, by chance, Lord Cornbury, now Governor of New Jersey as well as New York, happened to be visiting. Hill came to under the stern of Cornbury's ship, and went ashore to tell his Lordship what had happened. When Evans came up, sword in hand, and ordered the *Philadelphia's* master carried off to jail, Cornbury intervened, lectured Evans on his presumption in laying hands on one of the Queen's subjects outside his jurisdiction, and threatened countermeasures if he persisted in interfering with trade from upriver. Chastened but unrepentant, Evans went back to New Castle, while Hill saw his sloop off to Barbados and returned to Philadelphia in triumph.

Logan kept William Penn informed of the Governor's willful and erratic behavior. Even before the dramatic climax of the "powder-money" affair, Penn had sent Evans a pointed rebuke — with a copy to James Logan. When news of the firing on Richard Hill's sloop reached him, the patient Proprietor saw that John Evans must go. But Penn had seldom been able to act decisively or promptly, and now he found himself overwhelmed by his own financial difficulties, hounded by the Fords, and cast into debtors' prison. It was a year before he could appoint a new governor. It was Logan's difficult but not wholly unpleasing task to break the news to Evans. Even then, more than six months passed before the new governor arrived and Evans was finally relieved of his duties.

Captain Charles Gookin, Penn's new deputy, was a soldier, a scarred veteran of the wars in Flanders. He had not been in Pennsylvania long before he was face to face with the old problem of persuading the Quaker legislators to arm the province for defense. He soon learned how disastrously Evans had failed with his amateur stage managing, his crude attempts to collect "powder money" at the point of a gun. With Logan to guide him he resorted to tactics of indirection. There was no need now to manufacture a military threat. For on May 7, 1709, the war which had begun in Europe over the Spanish succession nearly eight years before finally came to the shores of the Delaware. Late on that day, a messenger galloped into town with the report — no false alarm this time — that a French privateer had landed a crew at Lewes early in the morning, had plundered the inhabitants, killed one, seized several others for ransom. Hard on the heels of this report came rumors of a great French fleet assembling in the West Indies to attack British North America. And to cap all this, orders arrived from the Queen that Pennsylvania must raise a hundred and fifty men for an ambitious expedition under Colonel Samuel Vetch to conquer Canada.

Logan was in his old dilemma, too consistent a man of the world to be a consistent Friend. When people asked him how Quakers could hang individual murderers and robbers, yet balk at resisting an invading force that would kill and pillage at will, he found it hard to answer. Gookin, however, was confident that he could find a hundred and fifty men able to bear arms if the Assembly would appropriate a substantial sum — say four thousand pounds — to equip and provision them. Logan joined him in proposing that such a sum be voted not as a contribution to the expedition against Canada but as a mark of loyalty to the Queen "to be employed as she shall think fit." The Assembly responded by appropriating not four thousand pounds but a mere five hundred pounds and stipulated that it be "put into a safe hand till they were satisfied from England it should not be employed for the use of war." Annoyed by the failure of his stratagem, Gookin angrily rejected the offer.

After ten years of living with a divided mind, James Logan now became clear on one point: strict Quakerism and government were simply incompatible. Loyalty to Penn and elementary political prudence kept him from expressing his opinion in public, but he made no secret of it in his private correspondence. He did not spare his fellow Quakers or waste any sympathy on them in their dilemma. "If Friends, after such a profession of denying the world, living out of it, and acting in opposition to its depraved ways . . ." he wrote Penn, "cannot be satisfied, but must involve themselves in affairs of government under another power and administration, which administration in many of its necessary points is altogether inconsistent with this profession — I say, if this be the case, I cannot see why it should not be accounted singularly just in Providence to deal to their portion crosses, vexation, and disappointments to convince them of their mistakes and inconsistency."

In this frame of mind he could only renew his advice to William Penn to sell his powers of government to the Queen before it was too late, before he was stripped of them by quo-warranto proceedings. If he could make a good enough bargain, he could rid himself at one stroke of both his financial and political embarrassments. True, this would mean liquidating the "holy experiment," but that vision had never fully possessed Logan's mind. Ten years of experience in "the ministerial part of the government," harassed from all sides — by royal officials intent on tightening their control, by Penn's own deputies straining after independent power, by an ungrateful, inconsistent people forever demanding rights and privileges — had shown him how many obstacles lay in the way of its realization. The people of Pennsylvania, for whom the experiment had been conceived, were, in Logan's mind, the chief offenders.

I V

Logan and the People

BEFORE LEAVING his province in 1701, William
Penn had signed a new constitution for Pennsylvania
which radically remodeled the provincial government.
Under this Charter of Privileges all legislative powers
were concentrated in a single chamber, an elective Assembly, representing the freeholders. There was no upper
house, such as there was in every other British colony, to
provide a check on the people's representatives. The ap-
pointive Council could only advise and assist the Governor; it had no direct share in the lawmaking process.
Moreover, Penn had yielded, against his better judgment, to pressure from down the river and added a provision which granted the Lower Counties, if they wished
it, a legislature of their own, distinct from that of the
province.

From the moment he first saw the document, Logan
had grave misgivings about it. He had no convictions
about the inherent right of ordinary people to govern
themselves and little faith in their ability to do so. Behind
the new charter he saw only the influence of men who
wished the Proprietor no good — the intractable Quaker
farmers and artisans of Pennsylvania, intoxicated with

the wine of liberty and craving more of the heady drink; the disaffected, polyglot people of the Lower Counties, fearful of being submerged in a Quaker commonwealth with whose ruling principles they had no sympathy. There was nothing new about these tactics; ever since they had first come to the Delaware Valley, the Quaker settlers had been pressing hard against the Proprietor's prerogative, while the people of the territories had long been restive under Quaker rule. Convinced that Penn had already granted away too much, Logan set his face against further concessions.

In the first trial of strength — with the people of the Lower Counties — there was little that Logan or anyone in Pennsylvania could do; and in truth, after the disagreeable experiences he had had with those recalcitrant folk, he was not disposed to exert himself overmuch. Penn had hardly sailed for England before they moved to claim their privileges under the new charter. Without warning, their representatives withdrew from the provincial Assembly, in which they had sat for nearly twenty years, and insisted upon meeting separately. They summed up their protests against Quaker rule and sent them to Whitehall, where Colonel Quary, prompt to seize any stick to belabor the Proprietary government, supported them. By the following autumn, they had decided they could not even recognize Penn's Charter of Privileges. Accordingly they refused to vote at the regular time for Assemblymen, and insisted that they could hold elections only by writ from the Governor. Special elections were held and eight representatives finally came up to Philadelphia. But they refused pointblank to sit with the twelve from the province. After wrangling for five days to no avail, they went home without ever having formally met as an assembly. Henceforth province and territories would be two separate governments, united only by a common governor. This partition of his beloved colony grieved William Penn deeply, and for years he refused to regard it as final. But Logan, who knew the temper of the people downriver, promptly accepted it as an accomplished fact and lost little sleep over it.

His struggle with David Lloyd, the tribune of the people in Pennsylvania, was to cause him, on the other hand, many a sleepless night. The Welshman was a tough, resourceful antagonist, more formidable even than Robert Quary. The Colonel had the power of the Crown behind him, but the Crown was three thousand miles away across the water. Lloyd had the people with him — the stubborn, freedom-loving Quaker farmers and a well-organized group of artisans who controlled the town corporation of Philadelphia. Lloyd and Quary had nothing in common except their jealousy of the Proprietary power; indeed, before Logan's coming they had been bitter enemies. But during Governor Hamilton's brief tenure of office, they had joined forces to question the Governor's authority. The arrival of Governor Evans, bearing a commission fully approved by the Queen, had undermined the chief basis of Quary's attack. But by the same token the new access of strength to the government gave Lloyd his opening to cry oppression and tyranny; now he could find abuses of prerogative, threats to the liberties of the people in every act of the Governor or the Proprietor.

Experience with the Welshman's tactics made Logan watchful, determined that the struggle, if it must come, should be joined on ground of his choosing. Penn's commission to Governor Evans could easily have precipitated a crisis, if Logan and his friends had not chosen to sidestep it. For that document contained a "salvo" by which the unpredictable Proprietor had reserved to himself a final veto on all legislation. The moment Logan saw this clause, he knew it would never go down with David Lloyd; indeed, he could scarcely justify a double veto himself, except possibly in affairs in which property was involved. The Council avoided trouble by issuing a declaration that the "salvo" was void, though this fact, they were careful to insist, did not invalidate the commission as a whole.

The Assembly, however, soon found another issue. Most of the legislators were farmers. They could not afford to be away from their farms for long periods in the spring and summer; consequently their custom was to meet for a few days at a time and then adjourn to go back to their plowing and harvesting. Governor Evans was annoyed by their independence, their coming and going at will. He claimed the right as Governor to prorogue and dissolve the legislature at his own pleasure. Lloyd and the majority in the Assembly protested, pointed to a clause in the Charter of Privileges that gave them the right to sit on their own adjournment. On this issue, forgetting their unplowed fields, they were prepared to fight all through the spring of 1704.

Unexpectedly, Logan himself gave them a new provocation. He had never reconciled himself to the provision in the 1701 charter which deprived the Council of its former legislative powers. Now that he had a regular seat on the Council, he was determined somehow to restore its status as an aristocratic counterbalance to the popular will as expressed through the Assembly. Only so, he conceived, would Penn's proprietary authority be safe. He drew up an amendment to the Charter forbidding the Governor to sign laws except in the presence of a quorum of the Council. No one could mistake his purpose to give the Council once more a role in the legislative process. The Assemblymen reacted at once: Logan's scheme, they declared, would destroy the Charter. Stubbornly they stood on their rights, grimly they defended the Charter of Privileges. All summer long they refused to pass any legislation of moment until they had fought off what they considered a tyrannical assault on their sacred liberties. The man they marked out as their chief enemy, the principal supporter of prerogative power, was James Logan.

If they had known what he was writing to William Penn that summer, their distrust would have been deeper, their indignation more intense. "This people," he complained in July 1704, "think privileges their due, and all that can be grasped to be their native right." Penn's liberalism had been too heady a draught for them. "Charters here have been, or I doubt will be, of fatal consequence; some people's brains are as soon intoxicated with power as the natives are with their beloved liquor, and as little to be trusted with it." Logan's ideal was the classical pattern of a "mixed," a balanced, government, an equipoise of three elements, monarchical, aristocratic, and democratic. It was an ideal embodied, as every educated Englishman believed, in the British constitution, and Britain's brief, unhappy trial of republicanism in the mid-seventeenth century only showed how democracy, unless blended with aristocratic and monarchical elements, would end in tyranny, the destruction of both liberty and property. "A well-tempered mixture in governments," he declared, "is the happiest, and commonwealth men, invested with power, have been seen to prove the greatest tyrants."

Lloyd and his partisans, though hardly democrats in any modern sense, were alert to resist anything that hinted of aristocratic privilege or prerogative power. Moreover, they were for the most part plain Quakers, zealous for their religious testimonies, austerely devoted to their sober way of life. William Penn's son chose this moment to break away from Logan's tutelage and behave in a manner that outraged all their political and religious prepossessions. It was already notorious among the older Friends that young Penn seldom came to meeting. Worse, he wore a sword and spent a great deal of time drilling the militia on Society Hill. For the militia was now finally in being. Governor Evans had issued a proclamation calling to the colors all who were conscientiously able to serve. As a special incentive he had taken it upon himself to excuse from duty with the town watch any man who would volunteer for the militia. This led some of the Churchmen to protest that they would not watch unless all were liable for service without exception. Hard feelings between the militia and the watch inevitably erupted into violence, and just as inevitably became entangled in politics. On the evening of September 1, 1704, young Penn and some of the militia officers were carousing at Enoch Story's Pewter Platter Tavern, hard by Christ Church. The watch passed by on its rounds. Taunts were flung. Fisticuffs followed. Bottles and heads were broken.

Two days later, the Mayor's Court sat to hear a charge of riot. On the bench as Recorder was David Lloyd, beside him two of his faithful supporters, Mayor Anthony Morris and Alderman Joseph Wilcox, all pious Friends, all enemies of Proprietary prerogative, all, as town officials, bristling with resentment at the Governor's unwarranted interference with the town watch. They quickly found that a riot had occurred at the Pewter Platter and cited William Penn, Jr., as the ringleader. At this point the Governor intervened and prevented the matter from going further, but the damage was done. Young Penn took the court's action as a calculated affront. Henceforth he had as little as possible to do with Friends.

He sold one of his Pennsylvania manors for ready cash and presently left the province forever in a British man-of-war.

Young William's escapade did immeasurable damage to his father's cause. The October elections faithfully reflected the popular revulsion. Lloyd's "country party" was returned to the Assembly in full strength. Logan, contemplating the vote, was at first inclined to attribute the result to Lloyd's talents as a "promoter of discord"; the people, he thought, "really design honestly, but know not whom to trust for their direction." But within a few weeks he had concluded that the majority of the Assemblymen were "knaves and fools." "It seems," he wrote Penn, "as if we were all in a ferment, and whatever was impure among the whole people rose in its filth to the top."

The occasion of these sour reflections was Logan's discovery of what had happened in the final hours of the old Assembly. The day before adjournment, the country members all impatient to go home for the harvest, the House had resolved to send a communication to the Proprietor, reminding him of the rights and privileges he had promised the people and complaining that he had not been as good as his word. Speaker Lloyd, Joseph Wilcox, and Isaac Norris were to draw up a bill of grievances. Next morning, the last day of the session, Wilcox reported that they had not had time to finish it. Eager to adjourn, the House hastily agreed on the subjects to be included, ordered the three men to finish the missive, and submit it for approval to a committee already designated to scrutinize and approve the minutes.

The House adjourned, and Lloyd proceeded, without consulting Norris, to draw up a bitter, intemperate diatribe against the Proprietor and his agents. He showed it only to two of his henchmen, signed it as Speaker (though officially he no longer held that office), and sent it off — not to William Penn himself, but to three prominent English Friends, George Whitehead, William Meade, and Thomas Lower, who were well known to be at odds with him in London Yearly Meeting. The "Remonstrance" — so Lloyd entitled it — did not spare James Logan. It accused him of "very great abuses" and "extortions," as well as tedious and unnecessary delays in the transaction of land-office business.

In Logan's eyes the whole affair was "a piece of the most unparalleled villainy." Norris, who felt he had been most dishonestly played upon, was just as indignant. He went to Lloyd in dudgeon to protest. Airily the Welshman brushed him off, reminded him that since he was no longer a member of the Assembly, having failed of reelection, he could do nothing about it. By a strange chance the bearer of the "Remonstrance" fell into the hands of the French on the high seas and was taken captive to France, where a fellow prisoner saw it and somehow contrived to deliver it to William Penn. Thus Lloyd's stratagem was prevented from having its full effect in England. But it did its work in Pennsylvania, increasing the bad blood between Lloyd and Logan, the acknowledged leader of the popular party and the man most intimately identified with the Proprietary interest.

The incident only confirmed Logan's conviction that Americans were incapable of ruling themselves. "We are generally in these parts," he wrote Penn, "too full of ourselves and empty of sense to manage affairs of importance, and therefore require the greatest authority to bend us." William Penn, weary of the continual bickering in his province, did not disagree: "There is an excess of vanity," he wrote to Logan's friend Mompesson, "that is apt to creep in upon the people in power in America, who, having got out of the crowd in which they were lost here, upon every little eminency there think nothing taller than themselves but the trees, and as if there were no after superior judgment to which they should be accountable." To Penn it sometimes seemed that all colonials concerned in government should be required "to take turns in coming over for England, that they might lose themselves again amongst the crowds of so much more considerable people at the custom-house, exchange, and Westminster Hall." Perhaps the experience would make them "more discreet and tractable," and hence more "fit for government."

By the following summer, however, the local prospect began to brighten. Lloyd and his supporters did not become more tractable, but the Proprietor's friends at last bestirred themselves, determined, as Logan wrote, to make "the strongest interest they possibly can to carry the next election." When October came, Shippen, Carpenter, Hill, and Norris all stood for the Assembly and were elected. Most of the other members, Logan reported, were "very honest picked men." Philadelphia County even passed over David Lloyd, though the town corporation, his pocket borough, proceeded to elect him. Bucks County, the stronghold of Lloyd's "country party," sent a few "scabbed sheep," but in general it was the best Assembly Logan had yet seen.

He found himself playing a new and agreeable role in politics. Everyone acknowledged him the leader of the Proprietary interest. He held, to be sure, no new office. That was not necessary. He had the ear of the Governor; he had a seat in the Council; his and the Proprietor's friends controlled the Assembly. He set to work at once feeding grist into a smooth-running legislative mill. He drew up a bill to settle the touchy affirmation question, and saw it approved, first by Evans and the Council, then by the Assembly — only to have it disallowed in the end by the Queen. He drafted laws to recover the arrears of taxes due the Proprietor, to bring order into the collection of quitrents, to improve relations with the Indians. The Assembly passed them all. Even Lloyd, whose legal abilities no one had ever questioned, acted for once a helpful and constructive part. When Logan sent Penn the laws enacted at this session, he generously added that their excellence was "chiefly owing to David Lloyd." If only the Welshman's heart were not so base, he sighed, "he might have been exceedingly useful." Yet it had been a productive legislative season, the first since Logan had been in Pennsylvania.

It was too good to last. By the summer of 1706, Logan's satisfaction had gone sour, turned to despair again. Once more the Proprietary cause was in bad repute. All the most solid Quakers were indignant at the immature and impulsive behavior of Governor Evans. He had staged his disastrous "false alarm" at the end of May. Before that he had committed another blunder by his callous treatment of William Biles.

Biles was a cantankerous old Quaker minister from Bucks County who supported Lloyd in the Assembly. He had made no secret of his contempt for the Governor. "He is but a boy," people had heard him say, "he is not fit to be our Governor. We'll kick him out, we'll kick him out." John Evans never forgot that taunt. Biles had been found guilty of seditious remarks and been ordered to pay three hundred pounds damages. The Quaker Yearly Meeting had required him to condemn his abusive language and promise amendment. Most Friends felt that this double humiliation was punishment enough, that Biles, a poor man, should be forgiven the heavy damages. But Evans was not in a forgiving mood. After promising Shippen, Carpenter, Hill, and Norris that he would take no action against Biles without first consulting them, he suddenly ordered the old man thrown into jail. Logan was horrified. How could a governor be so blind as to sacrifice all prospect of support by gratuitously insulting both parties in Pennsylvania? He went to Evans and remonstrated "with some vehemence, that he would find he had stabbed his own interest in the people's affections in the heart." But the Governor, tired of having Logan lecture him like a schoolboy, would not listen.

The results of Evans's folly were worse than Logan had expected. He had been prepared for a hostile majority, but not for a chamber all but unanimous in opposition. No friendly member of the previous "good" Assembly was re-elected; save for David Lloyd and four of his Bucks County satellites, the turnover was complete. The election, in short, was a disaster for the Proprietary cause — "the worst," Logan reported to Penn, "that ever I knew in the province." He and his friends would "use all possible means to make their sessions short and abortive," but he could not be sanguine. Gloomily he added: "I fear further remonstrances and addresses."

The Assembly revealed its temper at once by electing Lloyd its Speaker. Logan knew what this meant. Speaker Lloyd could be expected to wring every advantage from the Proprietor's embarrassments with the Fords, for Meade and Lower, the Assembly's unofficial agents in London, were close to that family of vultures. Lloyd himself was in a position, as the Fords' attorney in Pennsylvania, to raise inconvenient doubts about Penn's title to the soil and thus frustrate all Logan's efforts to sell lands or collect quitrents. Lloyd would be sure to keep a sharp watch on Governor Evans, rehearse and magnify every past error, exploit to the full every future misstep. Logan foresaw a dark and stormy winter.

The first clash came over the courts of law. The Queen

had recently disallowed an act of Assembly establishing a
system of provincial courts. Until a new act could be
framed and passed, justice was at a standstill in Pennsylvania. No one could collect a debt, enforce a contract, or
prove a will, and the jails were filling with malefactors
awaiting trial. Under Penn's original charter from Charles
II, the Governor had power — at least so he conceived —
to erect courts by executive action, by simply issuing an
ordinance. The previous Assembly had acknowledged this
power but had requested him not to exercise it; better,
they had urged, to let the people's representatives do it
by law. Evans had agreed. When the new Assembly
waited on him in October 1706, he reminded them of the
need for action and submitted for their consideration a
bill drawn up by lawyers and approved by the Council.

The Assembly, however, proceeded to frame a court
bill which bore little resemblance to the draft submitted
to them. It was a wholly new piece of legislation, drawn
up by David Lloyd, incorporating a radical departure from
colonial judicial practice — a system of courts quite independent of the governor. The Glorious Revolution of
1688 had given England, among other benefits, an independent judiciary; and David Lloyd, who could not
forget Penn's close friendship with James II, was clearly
bent on appropriating the fruits of the Revolution for
Pennsylvania. Under the terms of his bill, judges would
hold office during good behavior and be removable only
by the Assembly. Fines, forfeitures, and fees for tavern
licenses, hitherto perquisites of the Proprietor or his deputy, would be applied to the support of government and
the payment of the judges' salaries. And the courts, not
the Proprietor, would have final authority over land titles.
To Logan, Penn's land steward, this last provision was
peculiarly unacceptable, an outrageous invasion of his master's rights as absolute lord of the soil.

Governor Evans lost no time in rejecting the bill. He had no authority, he declared stiffly, to give away the Proprietor's powers and perquisites. If the Assembly did not straightway pass a law he could sign, he would have no alternative but to erect courts by ordinance. Logan saw the issue plainly, gave Evans his full support. Privately he vented his feelings in caustic language: the Assemblymen, he wrote Penn, were "vile vipers who swell with poison against thee and would wound thee equally deep in thy temporal and religious character." The Assembly, he was convinced, was determined to have "the whole power" in Pennsylvania, to "leave the Governor only a name." With the other members of the Council he submitted a detailed list of objections to the new bill.

The Assembly responded quickly: the Council was interfering, improperly acting in a legislative capacity; moreover, the Governor had no power to establish courts by decree, and if he should dare to do it, the Assembly would be driven to vindicate its own rights. The Council's sharp rebuttal, laid before the House on November 25, bore marks of Logan's trenchant pen. The Assembly, it said, should "consider that the business now is to serve the country at a pinch and not a trial of skill." A satisfactory answer was expected within twenty-four hours.

Five days later, the Assembly's message was delivered. It consisted of fourteen resolves. The first asserted the Assembly's right to impeach any officer appointed by the Governor. The next to last leveled specific accusations against James Logan: he had willfully concealed from the Assembly a communication from the Lords of Trade objecting to certain Pennsylvania laws; he had on numerous occasions given "pernicious counsel" to the Governor. For these malfeasances "he is deemed an enemy to the Governor and government of this province." The last resolve was a request to Evans "to remove the said James Logan from his Council and presence."

It had finally come to this: for his fidelity to the Proprietor, James Logan was declared a public enemy.

That evening, by flickering candlelight, Logan sat down and wrote to Penn. The charges against him were, of course, false, he said — so obviously trumped up as scarcely to require denial. True, he had temporarily withheld the objections of the Lords of Trade — on express orders from the Governor and some members of Council; later, when the Queen's formal message had come, repealing the laws, the objections had been duly laid before the Assembly. He had advised the Governor to establish courts, if necessary by decree, but the royal charter, he insisted, conferred that power beyond question; and, in any case, the whole Council, not he alone, had made the recommendation. Logan's conscience was clear. He was sure of himself, scornful of the Assemblymen. "As for my part, I value them all not one farthing," he told Penn. "Besides," he added meaningfully, " 'tis not me they strike at."

Penn would know who the real target was. Governor Evans understood perfectly well. He knew that to complain of "evil ministers" giving "pernicious counsel" was the time-honored indirect way of attacking men in power, of attacking power itself. It was time, he decided, to assert power, to put the contumacious legislators in their place. He ordered the House prorogued. The Assemblymen refused to go home, insisted on staying in session for two days more. They spent their time composing a new remonstrance to be sent to Whitehead, Meade, and Lower in London. Before they adjourned, they added injury to insult by ordering the provincial Treasurer to pay Logan's salary only *after* all other public officials, including David Lloyd, had been paid — if any funds remained in the treasury.

When the Assemblymen returned to Philadelphia two weeks later, they resumed debate on their court bill. On December 24 they heard a message from the Governor, taking note of the charges against Logan and refuting them, one after the other. Logan's own hand was plain in the message — especially in the sly suggestion that if it was "pernicious" to admit the Governor's power to establish courts by ordinance, David Lloyd was as much a public enemy as anyone, since he had openly acknowledged that power in the previous Assembly. That same day, Logan walked into the coffeehouse, where the Assembly's minutes were posted among the notices of stolen horses, eloping wives, and runaway servants, and took the minutes down. He merely wanted, he said, to get an accurate account of the votes for Governor Evans, but the House chose to see a guilty design to keep the contents of the minutes quiet. At once it appointed a committee — David Lloyd among its members — to draw up articles of impeachment against James Logan. The House then adjourned for six weeks, without taking final action on the court bill.

Meanwhile, Pennsylvania remained without courts. Early in February, 1706/7, unwilling to wait any longer, Governor Evans summoned the Assemblymen back to Philadelphia, demanded that they drop their delaying tactics and pass at once a court bill he could sign. To expedite action he agreed to meet in a conference to settle the points at issue once and for all.

The conference was held in the great hall of Edward Shippen's house on February 6. The entire Council and Assembly were present, but the discussion soon became a dialogue between Evans and Lloyd, two Welshmen with fluent tongues and quick tempers. At first, Lloyd rose

when he spoke, but presently began keeping his seat.
Evans reproved him, reminded him that it was customary
to stand when addressing the Governor. Lloyd replied
that the Speaker was "the mouth of the country" and
took orders only from the people's representatives. The
two Welshmen glared at each other. Was the Speaker
prepared to break up the conference over this point? Yes,
replied Lloyd, for he and the Assembly had been af-
fronted. Forthwith he and the rest of the Assemblymen
stalked out of the house.

Now it was open war. Evans and the Council refused
to resume negotiations unless Lloyd would apologize. The
Assembly, for its part, acknowledged that "standing up
whilst speaking before the Governor is a decent and con-
venient posture," but it refused to censure its Speaker for
behavior that was merely "inconvenient." On February 19, 1706/7, the Assembly threatened the Governor
with a direct appeal to the Queen. Before its note could
be delivered, a message was brought in from the Governor, repeating once more his objections to the court bill,
and threatening to establish courts at once by decree if
the objectionable provisions were not removed. Next day,
the articles of impeachment against James Logan were
read to the House. Two days later, the Governor issued
his decree.

Now at last, on February 25, the Assembly unleashed
its attack on James Logan. In thirteen vague, diffuse articles he was accused of "high crimes, misdemeanors, and
offenses." He had "secretly and wickedly" inserted in the
Governor's commission the "salvo" giving the Proprietor
a final veto, also the clause authorizing the Governor to
prorogue and dissolve the Assembly. His conduct of the
land office, his official behavior as Secretary had been
highhanded, irregular. On several occasions he had criticized the Charter of Privileges. Two articles rang changes

on the old canard that he had concealed the objections of the Lords of Trade to certain Pennsylvania laws. All this he had done "wickedly, falsely, and maliciously, to set a division between the Proprietary and the people . . . and to subvert the law, and to introduce an arbitrary government."

When the Council met, a week later, and heard the articles, it ordered the House to "prosecute the matter without delay, that speedy justice may be done either to the country or Secretary, and that he may not lie under the imputation of an impeachment without just cause." Logan then addressed the Council in his own behalf. The charges, he declared, were false, groundless, patently absurd. The political motive behind them — the cloven hoof of David Lloyd's calculating malice — stood revealed, he said, in the first two accusations — that he was responsible for the "salvo" and the proroguing clause. Obviously James Logan in Pennsylvania could have had no hand in drawing the commission which Evans had brought from England. He reminded his fellow Councilors how he had stood with them in urging the Governor to disregard these very instructions. But by their "malicious chymistry" the Assembly could extract charges of malfeasance from the most unexceptionable act of a faithful official. Clearly they were aiming beyond Logan at his — and their — superior. "There could not be a more flagrant instance given," he declared, "of their disaffection to their Proprietor and Governor-in-Chief, whose merit towards this province must in all ages to come be acknowledged."

The Assembly was in no hurry to bring him to book. Not till eleven weeks later, on May 12, 1707, did the trial of James Logan finally open. The proceedings were to be "as solemn and public as possible"; Logan himself had seen to that. They were held in Clarke Hall, his own residence, which happened to afford the largest room in town. The Governor presided, flanked by his Council. The Assembly attended in full force, Speaker Lloyd ready to act as prosecutor. A throng of curious Philadelphians crowded in as spectators.

Before the trial commenced, the Governor confounded everyone — except his Council — by announcing that he doubted his constitutional power to sit as a judge in impeachments, doubted indeed the House's power to impeach. Speaker Lloyd was caught off balance. Hastily he referred to the Charter of Privileges to show that the Assembly were the "grand inquisitors" of the province, specifically empowered to impeach criminals. As precedent he cited the impeachment of Nicholas More, Chief Justice of Pennsylvania, twenty-two years before. But beyond this he could not go. English precedent failed him. For in English impeachment proceedings the House of Commons were the prosecutors, the House of Lords the judges. In Pennsylvania under the Charter of Privileges, there was no upper chamber, no "middle state" between Assembly and Governor. For five years, in season and out, Lloyd had been reminding the Council that it bore no resemblance to the House of Lords, had no share in legislative or judicial proceedings. The Governor had temporarily outmaneuvered Lloyd, had caught the Speaker in the tight web of his own constitutional argument. Having disqualified himself as judge in an impeachment, Evans now exasperated the Assemblymen still more. As their Governor, he announced condescendingly, he was graciously ready to hear any complaints they might have.

Desperate to recover the offensive, Lloyd insisted that the defendant must plead to charges duly preferred. Logan now took a turn at baiting the Speaker. He could not plead, he said, for the charges contained "matters so unaccountable and inconsistent that he could not so much as apprehend what the Assembly intended by them." At the Governor's order, the articles were read. Then Logan made a little speech.

It was "no small unhappiness" to him, he said, to fall under the censure of the people's representatives. He spoke of the "particular disadvantages" he had labored under since coming to Pennsylvania — his youth, his inexperience, the heavy responsibilities he had been obliged to bear, especially as chief official of the land office, where he "had to do with a great part of the country in a matter that of all things is found to touch men the nearest, *viz.*, their estates." But he was not asking for sympathy; if resentment and spite were his reward, he would accept it. As for the charges against him, so far as he could make out their meaning he knew himself to be innocent. But he had, he said, "great reason to believe the design was not so much leveled against him as it was intended to wound another through his sides." No one in that great room but knew whom he meant. Let the House "proceed to the proof and explanation of their articles," he concluded, and he would "very readily answer to everything they could allege against him . . . but . . . at present, while he was so much in the dark, he could not plead regularly to them."

Ill-tempered exchanges followed. Sarcastically Lloyd protested that even though the Secretary "pleaded he was a minor, yet he should have more wit than to reflect on the Assembly." Logan retorted with stinging remarks about lawyers who "had the art of hampering justice, puzzling truth, and making easy things most difficult, all under pretence of law." In the end the proceedings could not survive a double impasse: a judge who would not sit and a defendant who would not plead. The trial

of James Logan broke up in confusion, never to be resumed.

When the Assembly reconvened, a month later, the
Governor declined to meet them. They spent their time
drawing up a new and strenuous remonstrance to William
Penn with a "catalogue" of his agents' sins, and dispatched it to Whitehead, Meade, and Lower. The charges
against Evans were familiar: the "false alarm" of 1706,
the "powder-money" episode and the firing on Philadelphia ships, the "frequent and notorious excesses and de-
baucheries" committed in the little cabin on the edge of
town.

There were two new charges against Logan: that he
had been privy to the "false alarm" and that he was
personally profiting from the sale of stray horses picked
up by his wood rangers. This last was serious — the first
charge of actual corruption. But the Assembly, having
learned that it was both easier and more profitable to
make accusations than to prove them, did not press this
charge. For the moment its wrath was deflected from
Logan and turned in full force against the Governor.
Even Penn's enemies in London were persuaded by Isaac
Norris, who was in England on business, that Logan had
been maligned, that if there had been arbitrary proceedings in Pennsylvania, it was the Governor, not the Secretary, who was at fault.

But William Penn, overwhelmed by his financial difficulties and languishing in the Old Bailey, could do
nothing about removing Evans and sending a successor.
So for a year and a half the province drifted, its government in futile deadlock. The Governor occupied himself by courting Judge Moore's beautiful daughter
Rebecca. The Assembly scarcely bothered to meet. All
this time, though James Logan stood accused of high

crimes and misdemeanors, no step was taken to press the charges or to give him opportunity to clear his name.

When the new governor, Captain Gookin, finally arrived, at the end of January, 1709, Logan found him "a plain, honest man and of a temper best suiting a soldier," obviously innocent of political experience, but apparently zealous and willing to learn. Logan could only hope his zeal and patience would continue, "for were he a Solomon," he wrote Penn, "he certainly will meet with enough to try his temper."

Captain Gookin soon had a taste of the Assembly's insubordination. On March 7, old William Biles and three other members waited on him at his lodgings to announce that the House was met, pursuant to its adjournment. Gookin was stiff and formal. In Her Majesty's other provinces, he told them, the Governor called the Assembly. Was it the custom in Pennsylvania for the Assembly to call the Governor? The members explained that by the charter the Assembly had the right to sit on its own adjournment. He was a stranger to their constitution, replied the Governor, but when he was ready to communicate with them, he would call them "in a regular and legal manner." Thereupon the House drew up a cool address of welcome, full of reflections on Evans and the "evil counsel" to which he had listened, and adjourned.

The Councilors read the address and immediately took umbrage at the phrase "evil counsel." Was the House referring to them? In April Gookin summoned the Assembly to Philadelphia to find out. He advised them to "lay all former animosities and jealousies aside." But he could not overlook their presumptuous slur on the Council. Quickly the legislators responded: when they spoke of "evil counsel," they had not meant the Council as a whole; they had meant one man — James Logan. In

spite of the lull of nearly two years, it was clear that
the Assembly had not forgotten its grudge against Secretary Logan. He promptly asked for a trial. The House
tabled his petition until it should have "more leisure,"
and adjourned.

But there was to be no leisure, for the plundering of
Lewes and the Queen's demands for military measures
kept the Assembly and the Governor wrangling fruit-
lessly all summer. Impatient to be in England to help
William Penn unravel his tangled affairs, Logan could
only chafe at the intolerable delay. Late in September,
1709, he petitioned once more for a fair hearing. The
Assembly's answer was an order to Speaker Lloyd and
Joseph Wilcox to draw up a new remonstrance protesting
against Logan's "neglects, affronts, and indignities" toward the House. This new remonstrance went beyond
any previous set of charges. It taxed him with calling the
Assemblymen "knaves and fools" (which he had done),
and virtually accused him (without offering evidence) of
taking bribes and embezzling public funds.

Logan postponed his sailing, set about preparing a
formal answer to all the charges hitherto leveled against
him. The language of his "Justification" was harsh and
blunt, heavy with sarcasm. He countered the Assembly's
vague imputations with hard facts, offering once again to
submit to prosecution "in a regular way" for any official
misbehavior. His vigorous defense of the Council's right
to advise the Governor plainly revealed the contours of
his maturing ideas about government. If the Governor,
he wrote, could accept advice only from the representatives of the people, "that image of monarchy, derived
from its original and glorious fountain at home in the
British constitution, which has been maintained in all
the dominions of that kingdom abroad," would inevitably
degenerate into a mere democracy. No doubt that was

what some people in Pennsylvania wanted — hotheads
who "thought that England never so truly knew liberty
as when some there proceeded so vigorously in rooting
up of grievances that with them they rooted up the royal
family and afterwards made themselves the greatest griev-
ance the nation had ever known." But sober men, Logan
was sure, would feel otherwise. Such men would know
that "the people alone must not be invested with the
sole, or what in this case would be next to the sole,
power in legislation here." Logan's dissatisfaction with
the Charter of Privileges, his rejection of its democratic
features, his preference for a "mixed," a balanced, government were now matters of public record.

From self-defense Logan turned to attack. By word
and act David Lloyd had manifested "an inveterate
malice against the Proprietor." He was guilty of "designs
invasive of [the Proprietor's] authority and right." His
record showed him to be an "open enemy" of William
Penr's government. Logan reviewed Lloyd's public career
from the time he had first known him, when Penn had
had to turn him out of his offices for defying the King.
He made the most of the "irregular and unparliamentary
proceedings" in 1704 by which Lloyd had "fixed on the
whole body of a people the overflowing of his own gall"
— the first "Remonstrance." He taxed Lloyd with sending
"gross lies" to Whitehead, Meade, and Lower; denounced
him for co-operating with the "treachery and extortion"
of the Ford family. Logan's indictment of the Speaker
was as concrete and forthright as the accusations against
himself had been vague and equivocal.

Governor Gookin ordered the Assembly to take up
Logan's charges: if they proved true, he said, the House
must consider whether Lloyd was fit to be its Speaker.
The Assembly simply ordered the old articles of impeachment read, then minuted that Logan's paper "contained

very scurrilous reflections against the Speaker," and resolved that his allegations should be considered — after all other public business was dispatched. A few days later, they adjourned for three weeks.

Logan now hoped to sail on November 12. Once more he revived his request for a trial. Once more he delayed his sailing, waiting on the House's action. When the Assembly finally considered his request on the sixteenth, it ordered him to plead in writing to the old charges under pain of being deemed guilty if he refused. Then at last, on November 22, the House took up Logan's "Justification." All morning and all evening the members considered Logan's defense, together with Lloyd's rebuttal, a lively rejoinder in which he called Logan a disciple of Machiavelli, "an incendiary and sower of discord," a prying busybody "very much addicted to a misdemeanor called eavesdropping." Late at night, they sent a messenger to Logan's lodgings to tell him he must appear at the bar of the House at ten o'clock the next morning to make good his charges.

He appeared as requested, but explained that, since some of his witnesses were not in town, he could not assemble them on such short notice. The House gave him until four o'clock. In a tone calculated to exasperate, he replied that he "intended to call about that time." While he was out, the legislators resolved (without any manner of hearing) that his criticisms were an offense against the House. Furthermore, he was to give an accounting of all the fines, forfeitures, taxes, and imposts he had received. Confronted at four o'clock with these resolutions, he pointed out that he had never collected any tax money, and that for the trifles he had received in fines and forfeitures he was accountable only to the Proprietor. "No ways satisfactory," the House pronounced his answers. Next morning — still without any formal hearings having been held — the Assembly declared Logan unfit to hold public office, ordered him committed to the county jail.

There were great comings and goings now between the Assembly chamber, Mayor Richard Hill's house, and the Governor's lodgings. Speaker Lloyd gave Peter Evans, the Sheriff of Philadelphia, a warrant for Logan's arrest. Somewhat timidly, Evans served the warrant. Logan persuaded him to go to the Mayor's house. There Hill in his old quarterdeck manner demanded to know how Evans "durst execute such a warrant" without first consulting the Mayor. Now Governor Gookin entered the controversy, ordered the Sheriff not to touch Logan. The Council declared that the Assembly had no power to arrest a Councilor, and the Governor issued a supersedeas. The Assembly pronounced the writ illegal, ordered Sheriff Evans to do his duty. If he should falter — so Logan heard — certain members of the House were ready to make up a posse to seize Logan. The poor bewildered Sheriff was now directed by the Governor to protect the Secretary from any attempt to lay violent hands on him. Balked and angry, the Assembly issued a final blast against the Governor and Secretary, dispatched a new appeal to its agents in London, and adjourned.

Two days later, on December 3, 1709, an impressive little cavalcade rode out of Philadelphia, escorting James Logan to New Castle, where Isaac Norris's *Hope Galley* lay at anchor, ready to sail for England. At the head of the company beside Logan rode Governor Gookin, former Governor Evans, Councilors Norris, Hill, and Preston; behind them, a "great number of gentlemen." It was just ten years to the day, Logan noted with a certain relish, since he had first entered Philadelphia, a humble, obscure youth of five and twenty in the entourage of William Penn.

V

London and a New Beginning

ON BOARD the *Hope Galley,* bound for England, for "home," Logan had ample time to reflect on his ten-year sojourn in Pennsylvania. On the whole, he had reason to be pleased with himself. Despite depression and wartime conditions, despite the people's resistance to the payment of quitrents, despite the Proprietor's own disastrous financial imprudence, he could give William Penn a creditable account of his stewardship. Though he had held no political office save his seat on the Council, he had contrived to keep the Proprietary interest afloat when the folly of Penn's own deputy had nearly shipwrecked it. And throughout his long contest with David Lloyd and the Assembly, though he had upheld the unpopular cause, he had emerged unscathed; the Assembly's failure to prosecute its charges against him was in itself a triumphant vindication. But there had been disappointments and frustrations. Among these experiences, the most bitter, because the most personal, had been his unlucky courtship of Anne Shippen. . . .

Anne was the daughter of Edward Shippen, the great merchant. Logan had fallen in love with her soon after he had come to Philadelphia, when he had lived briefly in Shippen's great house on Dock Creek. But he had a formidable rival in Thomas Story, Master of the Rolls, fellow Commissioner of Property, and Quaker minister. Anne preferred young James Logan to Story, who was twice her age. Her brothers, Joseph and Edward, were on Logan's side. But her parents, seeking a good match for their daughter, looked with greater favor on his rival. Story was a man of established position and undoubted piety, a "public Friend" well known in England and America. And Logan, what was he? A young clerk with no station, few prospects, and little religion.

When Anne, who had a mind of her own, refused Thomas, her parents were vexed, and Story, quite naturally, was mortified. In their disappointment and annoyance they turned against Logan. Story even haled him before the Monthly Meeting in 1703, and charged him, on the evidence of certain letters he had written to another girl, with breach of promise. It was only a few months since Logan had been called to account by the meeting for his proceedings in the affair of the Delaware island squatter. He was contrite, willing, he said, to let the meeting settle "all matters of difference" between him and Story. The meeting appointed a committee of its weightiest Friends to hear both sides and end the dispute. It took several months, but finally the quarrel was ended. Because the principals were in the public eye — one a minister, the other William Penn's agent — it was thought best that all the papers bearing on the case should be burned, all the pertinent minutes expunged from the meeting's records. Logan felt he had come out of the squabble at least as well as Story. "Perhaps," he wrote sourly to Penn, "[I shall] be as well received as a publican as he may be as a Pharisee."

Logan ultimately made his peace with Story, and the two men became firm friends. Nonetheless, the unhappy affair affected his disposition. People began to find him morose, peevish, sometimes overbearing. Even William Penn in England heard reports that he had "grown touchy and apt to give short and rough answers, which many call haughty." Often, when he reflected on the knavery of the Fords, the intrigues of his enemies in Pennsylvania, he gave way to moods of the blackest melancholy, the bitterest misanthropy. "When I consider," he wrote in the summer of 1706, ". . . the world we are confined to is capable of harboring so much villainy as should, one would think, be sufficient to infect the vital air we draw with a hellish stench, destructive to everything that's good or fair, I am quite sick of it, and could wish myself transported to any other better sphere — and surely a worse cannot be in a good and wise God's creation, except it be that infernal Erebus itself, whose powers seem to have broke from their centre, and to have full playday given them to range the more open and expanded ether which used to be accounted pure, but no longer will deserve the title. 'Tis horrid blackness all. . . ."

He was preserved from complete despair by two inward resources, acquisitions dating from his Bristol days as student and schoolmaster. In April 1708 he secured from England a copy of Isaac Newton's *Principia mathematica* — the first copy known to have been owned by an American. With the help of Charles Hayes's *Treatise of Fluxions* he quickly mastered Newton's system of calculus. This was a world — the world of the mind — in which he could feel at home, where the defeats and vexations of public life could not touch him. Sitting at his desk, his mind moving easily among Sir Isaac's abstruse concepts of fluents and fluxions, his pencil covering sheets of paper with the strange new symbols, he could console himself with a scholar's pride in an indefeasible mental possession: few men in America, perhaps no one besides himself, could use this subtle, complex instrument.

Secure in the citadel of his own intellect, he cultivated a Stoic philosophy of resignation, nourished by his reading in the classics of Greece and Rome. A man's happiness, he persuaded himself, must have "its foundations laid in the mind . . . must have as little dependence as possible on anything without." Foolish, therefore, he could conclude, to repine "because there has been a battle lost in Spain, because the enemy has taken our vessels, because injustice in the world prevails over right and equity, because the advantages we thought might have been ours are fallen to the share of others." All these things, after all, were "as far out of our power as the wind and the rain or anything that passes above us in the sky. . . ."

As he watched Cape Henlopen drop down below the horizon, he could put his disappointments behind him and look forward to what lay ahead — the opportunity of making himself useful to the Proprietor, of associating with great men and refreshing his mind in the stimulating atmosphere of London. To pay his expenses he had adventured twenty-five tons of wheat and flour in the *Hope Galley*, expecting to reap a quick profit in the Lisbon market. The *Hope Galley* was a vessel of two hundred tons burthen, just off the stocks. Isaac Norris, her owner, called her "the handsomest and best piece of work" to come from a Delaware River shipyard. There were two other passengers aboard and a crew of a dozen hands. Being a Quaker ship, she carried no guns.

It was well that the *Hope Galley* was soundly built, for her maiden voyage across the wintry Atlantic was tempestuous and exciting. For more than a week after leaving Delaware Bay, she was driven by hard northwest gales which carried away her foresail and main topsail, and sprang her foremast. For two days she scudded under bare poles while the crew labored to step a new mast. Immense following seas surged over the stern and drenched the passengers in the cabin. When at last the storm subsided, new terrors arose. Twice the topman's cry of "Sail ho!" brought fears of capture by French privateers, but both times the *Hope Galley* showed a clean pair of heels.

At length, after nearly six weeks at sea, the lookout sighted the Rock of Lisbon. But even now their mishaps were not ended, for an offshore breeze kept them standing off and on for three days, and when the wind finally shifted, they found themselves, to their mortification, not in the Tagus but in the Bay of St. Ubes, nearly twenty miles south of Lisbon. A pilot took them around the headland into the Tagus estuary and they finally came to anchor under the friendly guns of the *Dover*, a British man-of-war — only to have a press gang come aboard and draft two of the crew promptly into Her Majesty's service.

Logan, who was acting as supercargo, delivered the ship's bill of lading to the English merchants to whom she was consigned, and oversaw the unloading of her cargo. Then he amused himself by walking about the old, ill-smelling town, seeing its sights — the Royal Palace, the Exchange, the monasteries and nunneries, the ancient, many-aisled cathedral of Sé Patriarchal. The nuns of Santa Clara were "familiar in discourse, and very brisk in selling their sweetmeats, which they do," he observed, "at a high rate." "Their dress," he added, "seems exceeding antic, their heads being set off on both sides, not unlike butterflies' wings." He witnessed a procession of the Virgin Mary — the image "most fantasti-

cally dressed," illuminated by flambeaux in broad daylight, preceded by Negroes playing "most wretched music
somewhat like hautboys," and followed by the Augus-
tinian canons in their long black robes. The tawdriness,
the superstition, the squalor of the Portuguese capital
were shocking to a man accustomed to Philadelphia's
Protestant austerity, her Quaker neatness.

He did not wait for the *Hope Galley* to load with
wines but, impatient to see England, took passage in the
packet for Falmouth. He might have done well to wait,
for, almost within sight of the Lizard, the packet was
taken by a French privateer and the passengers carried
off to France. There he stayed for several weeks, waiting
for passage to England. Not till the end of March, 1710,
did James Logan finally reach London.

He found the city in a tempest of political excitement.
The Whig government had impeached Dr. Henry
Sacheverell, an outspoken Tory clergyman, for his public
attack on the doctrines of the Glorious Revolution,
especially the toleration of dissenters. Overnight
Sacheverell had become an idol and a martyr to the
Tories. Queen Anne herself had attended his trial, while
Tory mobs had clamored, howled, and, for diversion,
sacked and burned dissenting meetinghouses. When
Sacheverell received only a light sentence, it was hailed
by the Tories as a moral triumph. The furor was still
alive when Logan reached London. By day, as he walked
about the city, he could see the embers of meetinghouses
still smoking; by night, the jubilant flames of Tory bon-
fires.

Manifestly the times were big with impending change.
Logan bought and devoured every political pamphlet he
could find in the bookstalls. Everything he read strengthened his Whiggish prejudices, aroused his suspicions of

the Tories' "deep intriguing craft." Within a few weeks he saw his worst fears realized. The Queen, "weak woman," dismissed Godolphin, Marlborough, all her Whig ministers — "the most able ministry," Logan thought, "that England had ever been blessed with" — and replaced them with Tories, thus foreclosing, he was convinced, the chance of the quick end to the French war. The political overturnings of this mad spring and summer made a deep impression on Logan's mind. Some "strange fatality," he was sure, was at work in the world, addling men's minds, vitiating their politics.

Governments might rise and fall, Europe might be hastening to ruin, but James Logan had work to do. He had come to London to help William Penn straighten out his tangled affairs. Penn had aged noticeably since Logan had last seen him. "The effects of decaying nature through advancing years" were obvious, "the strength and brightness of his great genius" beginning to fade. With concern Logan thought of Hannah Penn's young family — Pennsylvania-born John, the eldest, was not yet ten — of the crushing weight of Penn's debts, of William Penn, Jr., and his proved incapacity for government. His practical mind could see only one solution: Penn must sell his right of government, relieve himself and his family at one stroke of a thankless responsibility in America and a heavy burden of debt in England. By midsummer he had persuaded Penn to take the first step — to submit a memorial to the Board of Trade, signifying his readiness to surrender the government of Pennsylvania to the Queen in return for "such a sum as may reimburse him of a reasonable part of his past expenses and relieve him from the necessities that his engagement in that province have plunged him into." The liquidation of the "holy experiment" was started.

But the surrender might take years, and meanwhile

Lloyd and his party, with their insatiable demand for rights and privileges, might wreck the Proprietary interest. It was time, Logan thought, for Penn to intervene decisively in the province's politics. At his urging, the Proprietor wrote a strong letter to Friends in Pennsylvania in the tone of a father rebuking his ungrateful children. He reminded them how he had created a haven of freedom for them; reviewed in detail the "licentiousness," the "turbulent endeavors" of the late Assemblies; referred particularly to "the violence that has been . . . shown to my Secretary." With Logan at his elbow to prompt him, he took up the Assembly's grievances and dismissed them, one by one, as trifles, not worthy to be mentioned. He would give Pennsylvania one more chance to redeem itself: "from the next Assembly," he wrote, "I shall expect to know what you resolve and what I may depend on." Should the coming election go as the last few had gone, he would be forced — no one would mistake the meaning of this threat — to reconsider his own "private and sinking circumstances in relation to that province." Penn did not tell his fellow Quakers that he was already on the point of opening negotiations for the sale of his government.

Logan spent as much of his leisure as possible with books and scholars. After ten years of Philadelphia's thin cultural gruel, it was like sitting down at a banquet table to be in London, the London of Addison, Steele, and the coffeehouse wits, of Newton and the virtuosi of the Royal Society. He passed hours of contentment browsing in the London bookstores; leafing through thick Latin works at Bateman's in Paternoster Row, where the books were piled in great heaps on the ground; turning over the new scientific treatises at Innys's in St. Paul's churchyard; buying and reading with delight the *Tatler*

and, later, the *Spectator* papers, as they came out week
by week; spending his "pence" on books, so he wrote
his friend Norris, with the same pleasure as others squan-
dered theirs on "pretty firesides." He made the acquaintance of two young Quaker scholars — Fettiplace Bellers,
a scientifically minded barrister, recently elected a Fellow
of the Royal Society, and Josiah Martin, a master of
many tongues and much curious learning. More than
once he took a wherry down the Thames to visit old
John Flamsteed, the Astronomer Royal, who was patiently
compiling a comprehensive catalogue of the stars at his
hilltop observatory at Greenwich.

William Penn, when he came up from his country
seat at Ruscombe in Berkshire, made his headquarters
at the chambers of Counselor Richard West, a rising
young barrister of Buckingham Court. There Logan met
a Massachusetts man named Jeremiah Dummer, who
had just been appointed agent for his province. A graduate
of Harvard with a doctorate from the University of
Utrecht, Dummer was excessively vain of his learning
and inclined to be scornful of anyone from Quaker Pennsylvania. Hearing Penn remark one day that his secretary
was a man of some literary attainments, Dummer formed
a plan to expose and humiliate him. He had a friend
in the country, he said, who had just lost a daughter and had asked him to compose a Latin epitaph
for her. Would Logan help him? Logan, suspecting
Dummer's motive, resolved to outwit him. He agreed
to write some suitable elegiac verses. Next morning,
he left them at West's rooms — carefully composed in
Greek, with four Latin lines to "excuse" his writing in
the older tongue.

He did not confine himself to London and the company of the learned. Isaac Norris had given him an
introduction to his wife's relatives, the Lloyds of

Dolobran and Birmingham, a family of wealthy Quaker ironmasters. Sampson Lloyd in turn introduced him to his sister-in-law, Judith Crowley, who lived at Stourbridge, near Birmingham. Judith was a modest, comely Quaker girl and Logan promptly fell in love with her. His friends encouraged him. Hannah Penn thought it high time he married and Isaac Norris in every letter to his Lloyd relatives loyally sang Logan's praises. Judith herself found her American suitor attractive — though she professed to be awed by his erudition — and the two soon reached an agreement.

But the girl's family raised objections — particularly her rich and ambitious half brother Sir Ambrose. Recently knighted, purse-proud and overbearing, Sir Ambrose regarded Logan as a provincial nobody with no wealth, no family, no social position, no prospects. Logan, desperately in love, proposed elopement. But Judith demurred; she could not go against the wishes of her family. "I dare not and cannot comply with thy request," she wrote. "I should, I am, and must be under subjection."

It was Logan's second disappointment in love, his second humiliation. He was resolved it should be the last. The path ahead was plain to him now. Somehow he must get wealth, raise himself in society, cut such a figure in the world that Shippens and Crowleys could not hurt him with their disdain. And this meant that he must go back to Pennsylvania. Up to now he had considered himself merely a sojourner in America, the temporary steward of a great man's estate. Now he saw that his future lay there if it lay anywhere. There, by diligence and shrewdness, he could improve his small beginnings in trade and, with God's blessing, amass a fortune. There he might some day live like a gentleman, be able to indulge his newly whetted tastes for literature and science. There, by virtue of his friendship with the solid Quaker merchants who dominated the Council, he could become a power in politics.

Already, so letters from Isaac Norris told him, the political atmosphere in Pennsylvania had cleared. Penn's "expostulatory letter" had arrived too late to influence the elections of 1710, but, as matters turned out, it had not been needed. Norris's skillful management and a popular revulsion against Lloyd's highhanded tactics had wrought a revolution at the polls. The Lloydians had been routed and the Assembly was now in safe, conservative hands. Richard Hill was the new Speaker, and Norris himself was sitting for Philadelphia. They had even solved the problem of military appropriations by raising two thousand pounds "for the Queen's use, to be paid to the Governor, and by him to such persons as she hath already or shall appoint to receive the same." Norris explained in a letter the rationalization that lay behind this formula and made it acceptable to at least some Quaker consciences: "We did not see it inconsistent with our principles to give the Queen money, notwithstanding any use she might put it to, that being not our part but hers."

Having caught a glimpse of a new and ampler future in America, Logan set about laying the groundwork for it in England. Land, he well knew, was the indispensable basis of social status. Land, he had every reason to know, was plentiful in Pennsylvania, and a potential source of great wealth. There were many Quakers in England who had bought rights to Pennsylvania land many years ago, when Penn had first announced his "holy experiment" — rights which they had never taken up. Systematically Logan visited these Friends and their heirs, bought up their "old rights." By this means he acquired claims to some seven thousand acres at bargain prices — thirty to forty shillings per hundred acres. When he got back to Pennsylvania, he could use his ten years' experience in the land office to seek out and patent desirable tracts for himself. There was nothing censurable, nothing underhand in what he planned to do; this was merely shrewdness. For the first time in twelve years Logan was beginning to concentrate on the main chance.

Yet he could not bring himself to be shrewd at William Penn's expense. The Proprietor had never paid him a penny for his labors as Secretary. But when Penn asked what he wanted for his past services, Logan considered his master's "melancholy circumstances" and asked only one hundred pounds a year. For the future he was to have fifty pounds a year as collector of quitrents, two and a half per cent commission on all other collections, and five per cent factorage on all shipments to England on the Proprietor's account. To strengthen his hand he insisted that Penn and the trustees under the mortgage give him specific authority to grant lands and collect quitrents. Armed with these powers, encouraged by the promise of a small but regular income, filled with a determination to make a place and fortune for himself, he prepared to go back to Pennsylvania. He would stay in harness, he told Penn, for two years, but no longer. After that he must be free to manage his own affairs.

On December 10, 1711, he said good-by to Penn and his friends in London, took a wherry to Gravesend, and went from there on horseback to the Downs, where the *Mary Hope* lay at anchor waiting for convoys. It was a month before the ship finally stood out from Plymouth harbor in company with nearly fifty sail bound for the Guinea Coast, the Canaries, the East Indies, or the North American colonies. After a week, the danger from prowling French corsairs being passed, the convoy broke up and the *Mary Hope* was alone on a stormy sea.

After two months of battling strong gales and high waves she made land off Cape Hatteras and started beating up the coast. It was the middle of March when the battered ship finally ran past Cape Henlopen, her crew and passengers on the edge of exhaustion, her provisions nearly gone.

James Logan was back in Pennsylvania, ready for a new start.

V I

A Buffalo Skin for
Dr. Fabricius

LOGAN HAD COME back to Pennsylvania determined to make money. Soon after his arrival he laid in
a specialized stock of English goods — blankets, guns,
powder, knives, cheap trinkets. William Penn had once
suggested to him that the surest way to wealth in Pennsylvania lay in engrossing the fur trade. Logan decided to
follow that advice. He would use his small capital to
import trade goods; he would supply them to the back-
country fur traders who dealt directly with the Indians;
and he would reap his profit by selling the furs in England. It was an opportune moment for such a venture
because the Tuscarora War in the Carolinas had temporarily disrupted Charleston's roaring skin trade and
given Philadelphia the opportunity to capture part of her
lucrative market.

The men he had to deal with — the traders on the
western fringe of settlement — were a crude, raffish,
violent lot — renegade Frenchmen like James Le Tort and
Peter Bezaillon; tough, hard-bitten Scotch-Irishmen like
John Harris and James Paterson; backslidden Quakers
like John and Edmund Cartlidge. For a man who had
only recently been associating with the coffeehouse wits

and learned virtuosi of London, it was distasteful to deal with such a "parcel of brutish fellows" as these — to sober them up when they got drunk in town, to pay their gambling losses, to bail them out when they were thrown in jail for disturbing the peace of the quiet Quaker town, and finally to attach their paltry possessions when they died, hopelessly in debt. But this, he had decided, was the way to wealth, and he was determined to have wealth.

In the pursuit of wealth he could be hard, venturesome, unscrupulous if necessary. In his own affairs he made it a sacred principle never to run into debt, but he regularly extended credit to his traders, because they had no cash and because he found he could keep them faithful to his interest only by keeping them in his debt. He charged them exorbitant prices for English trade goods — though he was constantly complaining to his London factor about the poor quality of those goods. He kept them well supplied with rum, though he was perfectly aware that there were Pennsylvania laws against giving liquor to the Indians, that the Quaker meetings disapproved of the practice, and that the Indians themselves had repeatedly begged the authorities to keep it out of their reach. The colonial fur trade was no occupation for overnice consciences.

The fur trade was, however, profitable. By 1715 Logan was shipping off furs to the value of one thousand pounds a year. Two years later, Isaac Norris could write that Logan had "found means to engross almost all that trade." Every spring and fall his warehouses on Fishbourne's wharf and on Second Street bulged and stank with deerskins, elkskins, bearskins, with fox, beaver, mink, marten, raccoon, and wildcat pelts. Presently he established a trading post on Conestoga Creek, one of the tributaries of the Susquehanna, and bought a wagon to carry his goods there and bring the furs back. He gave the heavy, lumbering vehicle a name, called it the "Conestoga wagon." The name stuck and became part of the American experience. Hooded with canvas against the weather, Conestoga wagons would go creaking and swaying through dark forests, over endless prairies, up steep mountain passes for two centuries, carrying generations of Americans westward. But Logan saw them, loaded with furs, sometimes five at a time, rumbling down the Philadelphia streets toward his warehouse. Before many years he would come to consider the fur business "a nauseous drudgery, to which nothing but the profit could reconcile a man of any spirit." But the profit, he had to admit, was considerable.

He might have kept all the profit for himself, but just when he had hoped to be free from Proprietary business, the Penns needed him more than ever. Word came from William Penn in the fall of 1712 that the surrender of the government was all but sealed, that the Crown had offered him twelve thousand pounds for it — enough to pay off the mortgage and give him clear title once more to Pennsylvania's soil. But at the same time there came disturbing hints that the Proprietor's health was failing. Presently a tragic letter arrived. Obviously written by a sick man, it began in a pathetic, querulous vein and broke off abruptly in the middle of a sentence. A note from Hannah Penn explained how her husband had been taken with a sudden fit of apoplexy even as he sat at his writing table. Soon there came news of another and disabling stroke. As a result the negotiations with the Crown came to a full stop.

Responsibility for Proprietary business fell entirely on Hannah Penn's shoulders, while her husband sat helpless, his memory gone, his speech obstructed, his mind clouded — only his indefeasible sweetness of spirit left to remind visitors of the old William Penn. Hannah Penn was an exceptionally capable woman, blessed, as Logan later wrote, "with a strong judgment and excellent good sense to a degree uncommon to her sex." But she had five children to care for besides the invalid, and she could attend to business matters only late at night, when her husband was asleep, for it distressed him to see her struggling with his problems and he unable to help her.

James Logan could not abandon the Penns now. He had turned over many of his routine chores to others — the clerical work of the Secretary's office to Robert Assheton, his duties as Receiver-General and clerk of the land office to James Steel, a young man who had proved himself as a quitrent collector among the refractory farmers of Kent County. But he still served the Penns as factor, and sacrificed his own interest to theirs. When it became impossible to make remittances in wheat — the Lisbon trade collapsed with the coming of peace in 1713 — he voluntarily gave them a share in his fur business. He credited a portion of every shipment to their account, and took his pay in country produce and provincial currency, claiming only his four per cent commission as factor. Somehow, he was determined, the Penn debts must be paid and Hannah Penn eased of her burdens.

Hannah Penn was appreciative of his services, solicitous for his welfare. She wanted to see him married and comfortably settled in Pennsylvania — for his sake and her own. In the fall of 1713 she reminded him that Judith Crowley was still single. But Logan had little hope in that quarter. He made one last overture to Judith. The girl's reply was friendly, but it was also final: she could not defy her family, she wrote; she must still be "under subjection."

James Logan was nearly forty. He longed for the comfort of a home, for a wife and family. Premonitory twinges of rheumatism and sciatica made him feel that he was growing old, that he could not wait much longer. His eye fell on a young Philadelphia Quakeress named Sarah Read — a girl not half his age, of whom, he frankly confessed, he "had never taken the least notice" before. Sarah had been well brought up by a strict Quaker mother, however, and her elder sister Rachel presided over the household of the rising Quaker merchant Israel Pemberton. "None in these parts," he decided, "could contribute more" to his happiness. True, Sarah did not have Judith Crowley's wealth or social position, nor did she have much education beyond the bare rudiments. But Logan was now "firmly resolved never to set up a gentleman"; he was prepared to "sit down and be content with ease and happiness instead of show and greatness."

Laboriously, he composed a declaration of love. "My dearest life," he commenced. "To tell thee how much I admire, value, and love thee and thy excellent virtues is needless, for thou canst not be insensible of it. I look on thee as one capable to bring a man the greatest blessing in thy person that he is capable of receiving in the world . . . and how eager one in my circumstances, who rates thee at the highest, would be to possess such a blessing may easily be judged." His pen moved slowly, for he was not accustomed to writing in this vein. Sarah, he knew, was a religious girl. So he masked his impatience with a show of devout submission. "I . . . resign thee up to that gracious God, thy tender and merciful Father, to whom thy innocent life and virtuous inclinations have certainly rendered thee very dear, that He may dispose of thee according to His divine pleasure, and as it may best suit thy happiness, humbly imploring at the same time and beseeching His divine goodness that I may be made worthy to receive thee as a holy gift from His hands. . . ." Should the Lord condescend to bestow her on him, he would accept her, he promised, "as a sure pledge of God's continued love to me, even after all the offences I have hitherto committed against Him, which in the course of so active a life as mine has been, have doubtless been many, and which in thy sweet company I shall endeavor to expiate, that linked together in a strong unspotted affection both of body and mind, we may also be further cemented together in the divine love that affords the most solid comfort to the soul here and the most lasting pleasure both here and hereafter."

So contrite, so pious, so touching a proposal Sarah could not refuse. They were married on December 9, 1714, in the great brick meetinghouse on High Street. His friends told him he had "never showed more judgment in any choice."

In December 1715 Logan's wife bore him a daughter, whom they called Sarah, and twelve months later, a son, named William. Now that he had achieved two of his desires — success in business and a degree of domesticity — he began to think about providing for his future comfort and enjoyment. He bought eighty acres of land out of town, where the Germantown road branched off from the highway to New York. Here on this Sabine farm, he promised himself, he would one day retire with his family, his books and scientific instruments, and give himself over to the pleasures of the hearth and the library.

Already he was beginning to collect about him the impedimenta of scholarship and devote his leisure hours to serious study. For the back yard of his house on Second Street he planned a small observatory and sent to England, to Joseph Williamson, the Quaker Master of the Clockmakers' Company, for the largest telescope lens and the most accurate chronometer that could be had. He had a scheme, he told Friend Williamson, for solving a problem that had baffled the greatest astronomers — finding "the parallax of our great orb, *viz.*, the earth's about the sun." Nearly every letter to his business correspondents in London, Amsterdam, Hamburg included orders for scientific and philosophical books — a new edition of Newton's *Principia*, John Keill's Oxford lectures on Newtonian physics, Pierre Bayle's great *Historical and Critical Dictionary*. "It may appear strange to thee perhaps," he wrote his agent in Hamburg, "to find an American bearskin merchant troubling himself with such books, but they have been my delight and, with my children, will, I believe, continue my best entertainment in my advancing years."

Humanist as well as scientist, he ranged far and wide in his quest for knowledge. "As the history of man has of late years been a large part of my entertainment," he wrote Josiah Martin, ". . . I would willingly know his humors in all ages and countries." So he set himself a course of reading in the history and literature of the Moslem world, which carried him from the Arab scientists through the *Historia dynastiarum* of Abu'l Faraj to the Koran itself. He polished up his Hebrew, dipped into Talmudic studies, read the lives of the rabbinical writers. Turning to another part of the world, he ordered books on Scandinavian history, runic literature, the Icelandic Eddas.

But the Greek and Roman classics were his favorite study. "I confess, as I advance in years," he told Martin in 1718, "the ancients still gain upon me, and the Greeks especially. . . ." The older poets and the historians yielded him most pleasure: "As they give us the only old accounts of time [besides the Scriptures]," he declared, "I am pleased to observe what the notions of men were at the greatest distance from me; for this reason Homer and Hesiod please me more than ever [and] Herodotus diverts me with some others. . . ." He could not rise above a certain Quakerish prejudice against works of the imagination, which led him to dismiss the plays of Aeschylus as "seven crabbed tragedies of no great use"; nevertheless he devoured every classical text he could lay hands on and sent off a steady stream of orders for new and rare editions, lexicons, and scholarly commentaries.

His insatiable hunger for ancient texts brought him into correspondence with the foremost classical scholar of the age. Johann Albertus Fabricius, Doctor of Sacred Theology and professor in the Hamburg Academy, was publishing a definitive history and bibliography of Greek literature in fourteen volumes. Logan faithfully bought and studied the *Bibliotheca Graeca* as it appeared, volume by massive volume (though he complained to Josiah Martin that the indefatigable professor had "much abused the world" by lengthening the work needlessly). Reading Fabricius's notes on Ptolemy one day, he came upon the statement that the first printed version of that great astronomer's *Almagest* was a Greek edition published at Basel in 1538. Logan was sure the learned doctor was wrong, for he himself had once owned an earlier edition, published in Latin at Venice. Unfortunately, he could not supply the evidence, for he had sold the book in Dublin before coming to America, twenty years before. He made persistent inquiries in Europe, but none of his agents could locate a copy of either edition. Nevertheless, convinced that he was right, he finally summoned up his courage and his best Latin and composed a letter to Fabricius.

"While from all sides, most learned sir," he commenced, "your sacred studies in promoting literature are interrupted by the sons of the muses and the priests of the mysteries, there can hardly be one or two perhaps from these American regions who claim your attention. Therefore allow me, since what is strange and distant wins esteem not on account of its worth but because it is unusual, to address you from the wilds of Pennsylvania." He introduced himself modestly as a student of the classics condemned for years to the countinghouse and the provincial council chamber. He spoke of his admiration for the works of Ptolemy, of his certainty that a prior edition of the *Almagest* existed, of his fruitless efforts to acquire either of the early editions, of his hope that Fabricius might be able to help him. With the letter, he sent a dozen choice skins from his warehouse as a present to the great scholar.

Fabricius in reply pointed out that even the Greek edition was excessively rare, not to be had for prayer or price (*nec prece nec pretio parabilis*). Then one day out of the blue a parcel arrived from Hamburg — the professor's own copy of the priceless Basel edition, a gift to the unknown bearskin merchant who studied the Greeks on the edge of the American wilderness. Overwhelmed by this generous act, Logan acknowledged it with the most suitable token in his gift — "an Indian dressed buffalo skin with the wool on." He did not abandon his search for the earlier Venice edition, however, and finally triumphantly located one — the very copy he had sold in Dublin many years before.

There were a few learned acquaintances nearer home who shared his love of the classics, his passion for science and mathematics. For a few years he basked in the stimulating friendship of Governor Robert Hunter of New York and New Jersey, "a gentleman of as refined a taste," he conceived, "as any we have known or perhaps heard of in America." For Logan, bored by Philadelphia's drab piety, its preoccupation with ledgers and accounts current, it was like being transported to the atmosphere of the London coffeehouses to be in Hunter's company at Perth Amboy or New York. For Hunter was a wit and a scholar and the friend of wits and scholars. Dean Swift and Dr. Arbuthnot had been his intimates. Dick Steele had sung his praises in the *Tatler*. He himself had written a witty, bawdy farce about New York politics called *Androboros* — the first play to be composed and published in America. With such a man Logan could discuss the subjects that really possessed his mind — not blankets and hardware, bearskins and beaver pelts, but Sir Isaac Newton's principles of gravitation, the physics of vibrating strings, the motion of a pendulum, the *Pharsalia* of Lucan, an Italian translation of Addison's *Cato*, John Gay's latest farce. Hunter sent him Latin odes of his own composition and Logan diverted himself by turning one of them into Greek.

Sometimes to their learned discussions the two scholars would admit a third — a young physician named Cadwallader Colden, recently arrived in Philadelphia from Scotland. Colden's intellectual interests were as wide as Logan's and his head was full — too full, Logan thought — of theories and hypotheses in philosophy, physics, and medicine. Still, he was a good mathematician with "a systematical head," and he won Logan's heart by admitting that he "admired the ancients above most other practical writers." Hunter coveted Colden's company too and offered him a post in New York as Surveyor-General. When Logan heard of the offer, he was crestfallen. He had grown fond of the young doctor, and if he left Philadelphia, there would be no one to talk with. When Colden asked him for a recommendation to Hunter, he could hardly bring himself to write it; it was "too much like a man's desiring his wife to speak on his behalf to another woman." "My heart," he confessed, in a rare burst of affection, "goes against my head." But, he loyally wrote to Hunter, if Colden were "doomed to quit Philadelphia, I should wish him at New York, and can say no further."

When Governor Hunter himself announced, in the summer of 1719, that he was going home to England, Logan's disappointment was great, though he tried to be philosophical about it: "Every pleasure," he wrote, "has its proportioned pain, and the higher our happiness rises, the heavier is the blow in losing it."

Happiness was a state James Logan had seldom confessed to. But he was happy during the years that followed his return from England. Secure and prosperous in business, blessed with an obedient wife and a growing family (a second daughter, Hannah, was born in 1720), surrounded by books and a little circle of congenial friends, he no longer considered himself an exile, a reluctant sojourner in a provincial backwater. He had struck roots in the New World, and he felt bound to preach love of country to his fellow provincials. As Presiding Judge of the Court of Quarter Sessions, he delivered a little homily on the subject in the course of a charge to the Grand Jury of Philadelphia County: "The lateness of this our settlement," he acknowledged, ". . . will scarcely allow many to account it their country, because they can remember that they were born and bred up in another. But," he went on, "while our estates and families are here, while our children are born and must subsist here, it becomes truly ours and our children's country; and it is our duty to love it, to study and promote its advantages." Family and estate, the strong ties of blood and property had made James Logan a Pennsylvanian, an American.

V I I

"Preserve the Iroquois"

IN MAY 1712 Logan rode out of Philadelphia with Governor Gookin and the other Councilors. They were on their way to the house of Edward Farmer, a prominent citizen of Whitemarsh, to attend an Indian treaty. It was a familiar experience for Logan. Ever since the Proprietor's departure, he had been the province's chief negotiator with the tribes under its care, the principal spokesman for Onas (as the Indians called Penn, using their word for a goose quill). Years of experience at the council fire, listening patiently to the interminable speeches, redressing minor grievances, providing the gifts which were the essential lubricant of Indian relations, had made him letter-perfect in the elaborate protocol of forest diplomacy. The Indians had come to trust him as they had trusted Onas himself.

Logan understood the crucial importance of Pennsylvania's Indian relations as no one else in the province did. England's war with France was approaching its end, for the plenipotentiaries had gathered at Utrecht to negotiate a peace; but the struggle for North America would not be ended, Logan knew, by any assemblage of diplomats in Europe. Its outcome would be determined at a hundred

council fires in the American forest. And the balance of
power in the American forest, upon which the very future
of the British colonies might depend, would be determined in the end by the attitude of the Five Nations, the
great Iroquois Confederacy. From their vast domain
stretching across western New York these powerful people
exercised sovereignty over many of the lesser tribes of
Pennsylvania and the Ohio Valley. They were the sole
guardians of the long exposed frontier between the British
colonies and French Canada. "If we lose the Iroquois,"
Logan had written long ago to Penn, "we are gone by
land."

The Indians whom Logan met at Edward Farmer's
house were chiefs of the local tribe, the Lenni Lenape, or
Delawares, fourteen of them, led by their headman Sassoonan. They were on their way northward to the country
of the Five Nations to pay their tribute. They were twice
subject, these ancient inhabitants of the Pennsylvania
forest — first to the Iroquois, their conquerors, who regarded them as women; then to William Penn, who had
bought their land and called them his children. Gathering
in a circle in Farmer's house, the sachems solemnly laid
out on the floor thirty-two belts of wampum, each conveying a message of submission to their Iroquois overlords.
Then they filled the long calumet, which Logan described
as a pipe "with a stone head, a wooden or cane shaft, and
feathers fixed to it like wings, with other ornaments," and
passed it to the Councilors that they might "smoke a few
blasts of it."

Now another wampum belt was produced. Logan recognized it at once. William Penn had given it to them
eleven years before with careful instructions that it should
be delivered to the Five Nations as a token of his "firm
and real friendship." Sharply Logan questioned them: why
had they not carried out Onas's wishes? Unsatisfied with

their mumbled replies, he ordered them not to return without assuring the Iroquois in unmistakable language of Penn's desire for a good understanding. To underline the message of the old wampum belt, the Council ordered a fine laced matchcoat of Stroudwater blanket cloth and a white shirt sent to each *royaner,* or hereditary chief, of the Five Nations. Ceaseless attention to Pennsylvania's relations with the Iroquois, Logan knew, was the price of the province's security.

Two months later, Captain Civility, chief of the Conestogas, came to town with a few of his headmen. Remnants of the once mighty Susquehannocks, now subjugated like the Delawares by the Iroquois, the Conestogas were a forlorn handful, huddled together in squalid towns near the mouth of the Susquehanna. Civility came in anger to complain about the misdeeds of the white traders, most of whom were in Logan's employ. The province, he said, had promised to control these men, had set up a licensing system for that purpose. Yet since the system had been in operation the Conestogas had found themselves "worse dealt with than ever, they received less for the goods they sold the traders, were worse treated, and suffered more injuries."

Logan in reply gave them a little lecture on economics, explained the elementary laws of the market. They must consider, he told them, that the object of all who engaged in trade was "to gain something by it to themselves." Every commodity, he went on patiently, "sometimes rose in price and at other times fell." Trade goods came ultimately from England, where prices were high because of the war. The Indians' furs found their market in England too, but though the English people were as numerous as the leaves on the trees, they were oversupplied with furs — furs that came from the Carolinas, from Virginia, from Albany, from Hudson's Bay, as well as from Philadelphia. Consequently, fur prices were low. They must not blame the licensing system, he told them, for that was for their benefit. The offending traders would be punished; but the Conestogas must learn to accept the vicissitudes of overseas trade. A little confused by their lesson in international economics, but reassured by Secretary Logan's paternal manner and inwardly warmed by a few glasses of rum, the Conestogas went back to the Susquehanna country to trap more beaver and marten for trader Logan.

Pennsylvania's Indian affairs were not always so simple. Within a few years international, intercolonial, and intertribal rivalries wove a complex net capable of entangling and frustrating the most skillful diplomatist. The ink was scarcely dry on the treaties signed at Utrecht before England's enemies were at work in the interior of the continent, the French tampering with the loyalty of the Five Nations, the Spanish egging on the Yamasee and the Lower Creeks to attack the Carolina settlements. Every exposed colony moved to strengthen its bonds with the nearby Indians who were under its protection. But every tribe had its traditional enemies among the neighboring tribes, and no provincial government was prepared to restrain its own Indians from sending war parties out, lest in so doing it alienate the people who formed its own first line of defense. Meanwhile, each government looked askance at its neighboring government and suspected it of stirring up trouble among the red men. Provincial jealousies and tribal rivalries fed on each other and the French had only to toss in an occasional bone of contention to keep the Indians at each other's throats and the provincial governments bristling with mutual recriminations. Two men — Governor Alexander Spotswood of Virginia and James Logan of Pennsylvania — saw the peril in this particularism and tried to forge a genuine intercolonial Indian policy. Their goals were the same — to create a common front against the threat of French aggression — but their methods differed widely.

In the spring of 1717 Logan heard from John Cartlidge, who kept his trading post at Conestoga, that there were murmurings of unrest among the Indians on the Susquehanna. Messages from Captain Civility confirmed the ominous news and asked for a conference. The governor — Sir William Keith, who had just replaced Gookin — hastened to the Susquehanna with Logan at his elbow to coach him. They found, when they arrived, that Governor Spotswood had sent a special representative to the conference. The whole frontier was aflame, tribe against tribe, and the French in the background were diligently fanning the conflagration.

At the council fire Logan and Keith heard an ugly story of murder and tribal warfare. A young Delaware hunter had been killed and mutilated by a party of white men and Indians "back in the woods behind Virginia and Carolina . . . beyond the furthest branch of Potomac." All the Pennsylvania Indians — Delawares, Shawnee, Conestogas, Conoys — were aroused, ready to seize the war hatchet. The next day, Captain Smith, the Virginian, asked leave to speak. Near Governor Spotswood's frontier outpost, Fort Christanna, some Catawbas, members of a tribe which looked to Virginia for protection, had been attacked by a party of Senecas and Shawnee. Smith had just come from Albany, where he had exacted satisfaction from the Senecas, one of the Five Nations. Now he wanted to deal similarly with the Shawnee. Keith demurred. It was not "necessary or useful" that any outside government should treat with the Indians under Pennsylvania's protection. In any case the Shawnee had no power to negotiate independently of their Iroquois overlords.

But Keith solemnly renewed Pennsylvania's covenant with her tribes, adding, for Smith's satisfaction, "that they must never molest or disturb *any* of the English governments, nor make war upon any Indians whatsoever, who are in friendship with and under the protection of the English."

It was a ticklish diplomatic situation with intercolonial jealousies superadded to intertribal conflicts. Governor Spotswood's fears for the security of his back settlements were not allayed by the Conestoga treaty. Logan could agree that it was no permanent solution. The frontier problem was an imperial problem. It could be solved only by a common policy, by intercolonial action. The Iroquois, he was still convinced, held the key to the solution. But New York by tradition controlled relations with the Iroquois.

When Spotswood himself came north in the autumn to confer with the governors of the Middle Colonies, Logan and Keith accompanied him to New York, where they worked out a provisional modus vivendi. A line should be drawn along the Potomac and the Blue Ridge; the Iroquois and their tributaries were to keep their hunting parties west of the line and the Virginia tribes were to stay to the eastward. If the Iroquois could be brought to agree, Virginia's outposts would be safe. Logan could not help noticing the difference between Virginia's and Pennsylvania's methods of dealing with the Indians. Spotswood was a soldier who had fought with Marlborough at Blenheim; he used the tactics of bluster, seeking to bully the red men into submission. Logan, on the other hand, had learned Indian diplomacy in the school of William Penn; he used patience, respect, the method of friendly negotiation.

He needed all his patience, all his skill in negotiation, all his imperial breadth of view over the next few years.

For New York's Indian policy presently fell under the control of the Albany traders, who were driving a profitable undercover trade with England's enemies, the French at Montreal. They refused to lift their eyes above their immediate interest, to see the Indian problem in imperial perspective. It mattered little to them if the Five Nations allowed their dependents to listen to French blandishments, to turn with hatchet and torch against the back settlements of the other colonies.

For Pennsylvania the problem was acquiring the dimensions of a crisis. Ever since the end of the war in 1713, crowds of immigrants — mostly Germans and Scotch-Irishmen — had been landing at Philadelphia and swarming out over the unsettled country to the west. Sometimes they took the trouble to obtain land warrants; more often they simply squatted. As the human flood increased, Logan saw the lands the Indians had ceded to William Penn filling up, the gap between civilization and the wilderness inexorably closing. Already at some points settlers were encroaching on the Indians' hunting grounds, their horses and cattle invading the Indians' cornfields.

In February 1717/18 Logan had ordered the Conestogas' fields fenced for their protection. Before the year was out, he was listening to the complaint of Sassoonan: white men were settling on his people's lands along the upper Schuylkill. Logan was able to quiet Sassoonan's protests with a few blankets and kettles, but he recognized the complaint as a portent. "Most of the Indian wars on this main," he observed later, "have generally been owing to their being wronged in their lands." But what could he do? So long as the Albany traders controlled New York's Indian relations, there was little hope of inducing the Five Nations to restrain their subject tribes or permit them to release more lands. Logan was driven to a temporary solution at odds with Quaker policy. He laid out near Conestoga a garrison town, called it Donegal, and manned it with stout men just off the ships from the North of Ireland, "such men as those who . . . had so bravely defended Derry and Inniskillen" in his own childhood. It was the first of many Scotch-Irish garrisons on the advancing American Indian frontier.

But he knew that this, like his other measures, was only a stopgap. No mere local or temporary expedients would ward off ultimate disaster, now that the Indians' lands and their allegiance were the stakes of a vast imperial struggle between France and Great Britain. But there were hopeful signs that the King's ministers were at last awakening to the peril. In 1718 Governor Keith received from the Lords of Trade a request for information about French activities in the West. What routes did they use between their colonies of Canada and Louisiana? What measures should be taken to safeguard British trade in the interior? Keith referred the request to Logan, realizing that he knew more than any other Pennsylvanian, more perhaps than any other American, about the subject. It was the kind of task Logan relished, a task which exercised his talents for scholarship and statesmanship. He studied maps and treaties, questioned his fur traders over glasses of rum. He learned most from his "greatest trader," Peter Bezaillon, an old *coureur de bois* who had roamed far westward in search of furs.

The French, he discovered, had several routes from Montreal to the Mississippi. He traced them all in detail, noted the locations of portages, trading posts, and forts, set down the distances "as the traders reckon them." The French, he warned, were "using their utmost endeavors to bring over all the Indians into their interest." The Five Nations formerly "stood chiefly in their way, but by their Jesuits and other means they daily debauch them from the English." Already seven hundred Iroquois warriors had gone over, and barely two thousand remained faithful to the English. The rest of the tribes in the interior — he called over the strange names: the Miamis, or Tweetwees, the Illinois, the Michilimackinacs, or Ottawas, the Sacs, the Foxes, the Kickapoos, the Osages — were friendly to the French, bitterly hostile to the Iroquois. The French could summon thousands of fighting men to the warpath, whereas "all the English to the northward of Carolina have not 1500 men in their interest, excepting the Iroquois."

How could the French designs be frustrated, the British interests safeguarded? Logan had an answer: by encouraging the fur trade. This was the Englishman's point of contact with the Indians, his best means of winning their friendship. French traders, Logan wrote, might "exceed us in industry," their *coureurs de bois* might be more adaptable, more "capable of the fatigues of long journeys and fighting by ambush in the woods," but "some of Virginia and Carolina," he observed, "have shown that they are scarce to be exceeded that way" (perhaps he did not want to suggest that the traders of a Quaker colony might also be familiar with the techniques of ambuscade). And the British had one decisive advantage over the French: their trade goods were both better and cheaper. Hence the Indians, if properly cultivated, "will choose to deal with us rather than with them."

Let the Lords of Trade, then, encourage the Virginians "to extend their settlements beyond the mountains" and even build forts on Lake Erie, as Governor Spotswood had proposed. Let them foster South Carolina's skin trade as a means of holding the Southern tribes. Above all — this had been Logan's refrain for nearly two decades — let them do everything to "preserve the Iroquois," England's irreplaceable bulwark against French aggression.

It was a masterly survey — succinct and exact in its

factual parts, shrewd and farseeing in its recommendations for policy. Keith embodied it almost word for word in his report to the Lords of Trade, who recommended it to the King as "the most perfect account" they had ever seen of the interior of America. Later, Keith published it in London as his own. It was the first accurate glimpse the English people had of the vast area behind the Appalachians. And its real author received no credit for it.

Gradually the Indian situation improved. Governor Keith went to Virginia and came back with assurances that the Indians of that province would respect the line of the Potomac and Blue Ridge. A new governor of New York, William Burnet, reversed the suicidal policy of the Albany traders. In June 1720, having occasion to be near Conestoga on business, Logan summoned the chiefs of the local tribes to a treaty which he conducted entirely by himself with great success.

In his opening speech he reminded them that he was "their old friend, with whom they had been acquainted in their treaties for twenty years past." The Conestogas for their part recalled the covenant chain that had bound them to William Penn and expressed their wish to "renew and strengthen it with their friend, who has always represented William Penn to them since he left them." Logan's response was carefully phrased in the traditional rhetoric of the council fire: "This chain has been made near forty years ago. It is at this time strong and bright as ever, and I hope will continue so between our children and your children, and their children's children to all generations, while the water flows or the sun shines in the heavens."

Then, without dropping the fatherly tone, he read them a lesson in international politics. They were wrong to let their young men go out on war parties with the Iroquois against the Southern tribes. Young men, he knew, "love to go sometimes to war to show their manhood, but they have unhappily gone against Indians that are in friendship with the English." Every Indian understood how the Mohawks, Oneidas, Cayugas, Onondagas, and Senecas were united to form the Five Nations. "So the English," said Logan, "though they have different governments, and are divided into New England, New York, New Jersey, Pennsylvania, Maryland, Virginia, and Carolina, yet they are all under one great king, who has twenty times as many subjects as all these, and has in one city as many subjects as all the Indians that we know in North America. To him we are all subject and are all governed by the same laws." Therefore, he explained, "those Indians who are in league with one government are in league with all. Your friendship with us recommends you to the friendship of all other English governments, and their friends are our friends. You must not, therefore, hunt or annoy any of the English or any of their friends whatsoever."

Having unfolded to the chiefs their obligations as allies of Pennsylvania, he ended his lesson by explaining the designs of the French. "I must further inform you, as your friend, that this whole business of making war in the manner you do is now owing to those who desire nothing more than to see all the Indians cut off, as well to the northward as to the southward, that is, the French of Canada, for they would have the Five Nations destroy the southern Indians, and the southern Indians destroy you and the Five Nations, the destruction of all being their desire."

His lecture had its effect. The Indians agreed to send wampum belts to the Governor of Virginia "to assure him of their resolution to live in peace and to desire him to acquaint all his Indians with the same.''

Soon there came an unexpected opportunity to negotiate directly with the Iroquois. In June 1721 word came that sachems of three Iroquois nations were at Conestoga asking for a parley with the Pennsylvanians. It was unseasonably hot and Logan was suffering from a crippling attack of rheumatism. Still, he could not miss this chance to meet face to face with the chiefs whose word was the law of the Pennsylvania forest. So, with Sarah in the chaise to nurse him, he jolted over the road to Conestoga behind Governor Keith and four other Councilors.

The conference was a brilliant success. The Iroquois, to everyone's surprise, were cordial and friendly. Keith, with the ailing Logan to put words in his mouth, managed the negotiations superbly. The chain of friendship which William Penn had forged many years before was scoured of its rust and brightened. At the end of the treaty Keith gave the Indians a gold coronation medal bearing the likeness of George I "as a token that an entire and lasting friendship is now established forever between the English in this country and the great Five Nations."

Late in the summer of 1722, Governor Keith journeyed to Albany with Governor Burnet of New York and Governor Spotswood of Virginia for a plenary council with the Iroquois Confederacy. It was to be the most brilliant and comprehensive Indian conference yet held in British America — on one side, in their bright-colored ceremonial dress, the *royaners* of the Six Nations (the Tuscaroras had recently been admitted to the confederacy); on the other, the three provincial governors in resplendent uniforms, surrounded by members of their councils. Both the Indians and the Pennsylvania Assembly wanted Logan at the council fire, but Sarah was about to be brought to bed with her fifth child and so he reluctantly stayed behind.

This conference was as successful as the last one. Spotswood blustered as usual and drew from the Indians a promise to keep their hunting parties on the far side of the mountains. Keith, schooled by Logan in the techniques of Quaker diplomacy, won the Indians' confidence with a mild and friendly speech and put them in a frame of mind to renew the covenant chain, this time with all the British colonies. Though Logan was not present at the conference, its outcome was a triumph for the policy he had been urging for twenty years, a policy based on one imperative: "preserve the Iroquois." With the Albany treaty of 1722 Pennsylvania came into its own as the keystone of a strong defensive system and James Logan emerged as an intercolonial statesman of imperial vision.

V I I I

"A Wilderness of Briars and Thorns"

On July 30, 1718, after six years of half life, William Penn died at Ruscombe. The news reached Logan in the autumn. It was like a rumble of distant thunder, portending a new storm, a new period of political turbulence and uncertainty for Pennsylvania. White man and red mourned his passing. The Indians, to whom Onas had been as a father, sent his widow a bundle of skins to clothe her in her journey through the rough wilderness that lay ahead. "For my own part," Hannah Penn wrote Logan, "I expect a wilderness of briars and thorns here, as transplanted from thence, which whether I shall be able to grabble through without the help of my friends I have great reason to question, notwithstanding the Indians' present, which I now want to put on, having the woods and wilderness to travel through indeed." The Proprietor's death revived in new and sharper form all the thorny issues of earlier days — the location of the power of government, the security of land titles, the powers of the governor, the privileges of the people. If Logan cherished any thoughts of retiring from public life, sympathy for William Penn's widow caused him to put them aside.

Penn's will, written in 1712, in the shadow of his long last illness, raised more questions than it settled. He had devised the government of Pennsylvania in trust to two highly placed noblemen, Robert Harley, Earl of Oxford, and John, Earl Poulett, with instructions to sell it to the Queen or anyone else who would buy. Now, in 1718, William Penn being dead and the sale still unconsummated, no one could say to whom the government belonged. To Harley and Poulett as trustees? To William Penn, Jr., as eldest son and heir-at-law? To Hannah Penn on behalf of her minor children, to whom the title to Pennsylvania's soil had been bequeathed? Or to the Crown by virtue of Penn's express intention to sell? For a time Logan favored William Penn, Jr., though the people of Pennsylvania, who remembered the young scapegrace too well, refused to hear of his pretensions. But soon William, Jr., was dead too, worn out by his own excesses. Logan then transferred his support to Hannah Penn, who had instituted an amicable Exchequer suit with Springett Penn, the son of William, Jr., to determine where the right of government lay.

There were ominous rumblings closer at hand. In the Lower Counties the old agitation for a royal government revived. Moreover, there were rumors from England that the Earl of Sutherland was trying to gain control of the territories by exposing an undoubted defect in Penn's title deed: the Duke of York, back in 1682, had deeded the lands on the lower Delaware to Penn before he had actually received the grant from his royal brother Charles II. And to make bad matters incalculably worse, the house of Baltimore was pressing its old claims again. Not only were its agents presuming to sell lands between Chesapeake and Delaware which Logan believed to have been granted to William Penn, selling them at one fifth the price Logan was charging, they were even sending their surveyors up into the Nottingham region, ten miles above the head of Chesapeake Bay, where Logan had planted a settlement of Pennsylvanians.

Only Logan seemed to realize how much was at stake in the unsettled boundary disputes. According to an Order-in-Council of 1685, confirmed by Queen Anne in 1709, the peninsula between Chesapeake and Delaware bays was to be divided north and south at the midpoint of a line run due west from Cape Henlopen, and Baltimore was to have the area to the west and south, down to the Virginia line. But a line run west from Cape Henlopen, Logan was aware, would throw the flourishing little port of Lewes into Baltimore's hands. The situation north of the Chesapeake was even more desperate. Baltimore's charter of 1632 had fixed, and Penn's charter of fifty years later had assumed, an east-west division line at the fortieth parallel. No one had known then and no one knew now precisely where the fortieth parallel lay. But Logan was beginning to suspect — and with good reason — that it might be found to lie several miles north of Philadelphia! If so, Penn's capital and all the rich, rolling farmlands of Chester County would be lost. And none of the Penns — neither Hannah, who was overwhelmed with domestic cares, nor her sons, who were still under age — could be brought to give the matter a thought!

Logan had given it a great deal of thought. He had spent hours, days, weeks poring over the charters, studying old books of history and geography, scrutinizing old maps, desperately seeking evidence that the documents did not mean what they seemed to say. The "fortieth degree" of the charters, he concluded, could not possibly be the actual fortieth degree of latitude; that would make nonsense of other provisions in the documents. In the granting and confirming of the charters it had always been assumed that the fortieth parallel lay somewhere near the head of Chesapeake Bay, roughly in the latitude of New Castle. That, after all, was where Captain John Smith's well-known map of 1624 had shown it. And that was where everyone concerned with the charters had believed it to fall — Charles I, who had granted Maryland, and the first Lord Baltimore, who had received it; Charles II, who had granted Pennsylvania, and William Penn, who had received it; James II and Queen Anne, who had successively confirmed Penn's grant. Where the parallel might ultimately be found to lie when accurate instruments were used was immaterial, Logan concluded, in view of these undoubted historical facts.

It was a harder task to work out a historical claim to the region south of Lewes, but Logan was equal to it. He remembered having once seen an old Dutch map on which the name Henlopen was attached to a "false cape" nearly twenty miles below the one that now bore the name. It was this map, Penn had told him, that the Privy Council had used in 1685 when it fixed the boundaries of the Lower Counties. If Logan could only find that map, he might save thousands of acres.

After months of searching and inquiring, he finally found one — not the map Penn had shown him, to be sure, but one which served equally well — an old Dutch map that gave the name Henlopen to the more southerly cape.

In triumph he assembled his evidence, set it forth cogently in a paper which he called "The Claims of the Proprietors of Maryland and Pennsylvania Stated," and sent it off to Hannah Penn with the suggestion that she submit it to the Board of Trade. Another copy went to the Assembly of the territories. The Assemblymen had voted him their thanks and sent copies into each of the three counties to reassure the anxious freemen that their land titles were secure. But Hannah Penn and her advisers in England had done nothing.

They might ignore this overhanging threat to the Penn property, but they could not in the end overlook the dangerous insubordination of Deputy-Governor William Keith. A Scotsman, about to fall heir to a baronetcy, Keith had come to the colonies as Surveyor-General of the Customs in succession to Robert Quary. Suddenly removed from office in 1716 on suspicion of Jacobitism, he had gone back to England, taking with him not only the Pennsylvania Council's "favorable opinion of his good sense, sweetness of disposition, and moderation," but also their unanimous recommendation that he be made governor in place of Charles Gookin. Gookin, who had once seemed so sober and sensible after the immaturities of John Evans, had turned out in the end to be a hopeless misfit — stupid, overbearing, consumed by jealousy and avarice, subject to recurrent fits of insanity, and, all in all, Logan concluded, "the weakest animal that was ever called a Governor." (Andrew Hamilton, a brilliant lawyer recently arrived in Philadelphia and not inhibited by Quaker scruples, had expressed his contempt for Gookin and his highhanded conduct in stronger language: "Damn him," he had burst out, "if I ever meet the damned dog Gookin out of the province . . . by the eternal God I will pistol him; he deserves to be shot or ripped open for what he has done.") William Penn himself, in one of his last official acts, had signed Keith's commission in a shaky hand, and the new governor with his family had arrived in Philadelphia at the end of May, 1717. Handsome, self-assured, affable, intelligent, Keith quickly won the support of every faction in the colony — for his predecessor, with fine impartiality, had antagonized them all. Soon Logan and his circle were speaking in the highest terms of Keith's "skill and good genius" for government, his "humanity and freedom of access," his "professed good will to the people of this province."

But in these very qualities of political skill, humanity, and sympathy with the people lurked a danger to the Proprietary authority that Logan could not long overlook. Under the Charter of Privileges political power was divided between the Proprietor and the people. The governor represented the Proprietor, the Assembly the people. But what if a governor should make common cause with the people — who then would speak for the Proprietor? Logan had always considered the Charter of Privileges radically defective because it provided no check on the governor. The Council could only advise and assist, and Keith had not been in office a year before he showed how little he felt bound to take its advice. At a meeting in February 1717/18, a majority of the Councilors objected to some bills passed by the Assembly, but Keith signed them into law over their protest. Logan, Richard Hill, and Jonathan Dickinson quit the council chamber while he signed, "lest their presence . . . might be understood to carry their assent along with it." The breach was soon healed, but it left a tiny scar on the memory. Keith was obviously a man of superior talents, an able and efficient administrator, unlike his predecessors. But he was obviously a man of strong will too, impatient of restraint, a clever opportunist who could wring private advantage from the distress of the people and the Proprietor alike. By 1721 issues were beginning to arise on which the Governor openly took the side of the Assembly against the Council, against Logan and the Proprietor's friends.

Hard times prepared the soil from which the issues sprang. The prosperity which had followed the peace of

Utrecht gave way after a few years to depression. The fantastic South Sea Bubble burst in 1720, setting off a financial panic in London, and transatlantic trade suffered in consequence. The market for Logan's furs declined so much that he thought seriously of retiring to his plantation outside the city and getting his living "directly from the earth." By 1721 gold and silver had disappeared from circulation, the precious trade with the West Indies had collapsed, most of Philadelphia's shipping was tied up at wharfside, and the commerce of the Delaware Valley was at a standstill.

When the farmer brought his produce to the Philadelphia merchant, he got little or nothing for it. When he applied to the same merchant for a loan to tide him over the winter, he was obliged to pay eight per cent interest. Naturally, he blamed the merchant for all his woes. Politics quickly reflected the rising resentment. The autumn elections of 1721, Logan observed, were "very mobbish and carried by a levelling spirit." Isaac Norris, Richard Hill, Jonathan Dickinson—merchants and old friends of the Proprietor — were turned out, their seats taken by men of a different stamp — men like Joshua Carpenter and Francis Rawle, who had sat in the Assembly which had impeached James Logan fifteen years before. If this turn of events was ominous, the Governor's reaction was more so. In addressing the new Assembly, he took special note of the overturn, and showed how accurately he had gauged its meaning. Shrewdly he appealed to the temper of the new house with flattering references to "that simplicity or rectitude of mind which . . . is the poor man's greatest ornament." "Most certainly," he assured the lawmakers, "the Governor's true interest and the honor and reputation of an Assembly will always be found inseparable."

A few weeks later, while the Assembly was in recess

for the fall plowing, a small anonymous book appeared
with the title *Some Remedies Proposed for Restoring the
Sunk Credit of the Province of Pennsylvania.* It was an
able and witty tract. People promptly ascribed it to
Assemblyman Francis Rawle, a Philadelphia Friend of
wide reading and popular sympathies. The main remedy
he prescribed for Pennsylvania's economic ills was one
which New England and the Carolinas had been taking
for years: paper money — bills of credit issued by the
Assembly on the security of land. Let the dose be
moderate and carefully administered, Rawle advised,
and Pennsylvania's languishing economy could be expected to revive promptly with no risk of harmful side
effects.

The country folk, foreseeing higher prices for their produce and easy credit from the land bank, greeted Rawle's
prescription with enthusiasm. The merchants shuddered,
recalling the recent experience of South Carolina, where
overindulgence in this agreeable remedy had led to depreciation and financial chaos. For the moment Keith
straddled. He urged the Assembly to find some method
to "restore the planter's credit without discouraging the
merchant by whose industry alone our trade must be
supported. . . ."

Meanwhile the depression deepened. Houses stood vacant in Philadelphia; some of the "poorer sort" were
leaving town in search of employment elsewhere. The
people grew more restless, more rebellious, more openly
critical of the "designing persons" whom they accused of
profiting from their distress. Their criticism was aimed
chiefly at the Commissioners of Property, who controlled
land sales, the merchants, who controlled credit, the
Councilors, who sought to control the Governor, and the
judges, who controlled the processes of the law. Inevitably James Logan — Commissioner of Property, mer-

chant, Councilor, justice of the county court, and an old
enemy to boot — bore the brunt of their resentment.

On April 16, 1722, at a stormy Council meeting,
Keith finally showed his hand. The immediate point at
issue was a complicated one: it involved the Pennsylvania
Indians and the troublesome boundary dispute with
Maryland, but it also involved the prestige and authority
of the Commissioners of Property, of the Council, and,
more especially, of James Logan. Keith was just back
from Conestoga and the Susquehanna country. Rumors of
a copper mine on the far side of the river had attracted
prospectors from Pennsylvania and Maryland. The
Indians were disturbed to see white men prowling about
on land which still belonged to them. The Council was
alarmed at the presence of Marylanders so far north.
Governor Keith had gone to Conestoga to quiet the
Indians, to warn the invaders off — and, incidentally,
have the copper mine surveyed for himself. Logan had
got wind of the Governor's move and sent James Steel
off post haste to the Susquehanna with orders to survey
the land in the name of the Commissioners. Logan was
determined, if the mine should turn out to be profitable,
that the Penn family should benefit.

Keith was irate. In the council chamber on April 16
he turned on Logan, Norris, and Hill, the Commissioners of Property. Peremptorily, he demanded to know
whether Steel had acted under their orders. Yes, replied
the Commissioners, and they would answer for his actions. Surveys, after all, were their responsibility. Neither
the Governor nor the Council had any jurisdiction in
matters of property. Useless for Keith to insist that he
was charged with keeping the peace, that he had acted
to quiet the Indians, to prevent incursions from Maryland. The Commissioners stood their ground, and Keith

left the meeting speechless with anger, determined to pursue his own course.

In June he was back at Conestoga in council with the Indians. He moved rapidly now, for there was disturbing news from the south. Two Pennsylvania officials had been arrested and imprisoned by the Maryland authorities while doing their duty in the Nottingham lots. It looked as if Maryland were launching a concerted campaign of aggression all along the disputed boundary line. Keith quickly agreed with the Indians that his surveyors should lay out a large manor across the Susquehanna in the name of Springett Penn. He also ordered a company of militia from New Castle County to the mouth of Octoraro Creek, below Conestoga, where he proposed to run a boundary line unilaterally. Then he notified his Council by letter what he had done.

The Council met on June 20. In the security of Philadelphia, sixty-five miles from the frontier, they felt little of the urgency that had stirred Keith to action. Coolly they declined to accept any responsibility "as a Council of State" for the Governor's surveys. They did not tell the Governor he lacked authority to make them; they merely referred him to his instructions from the Proprietor. As for running a boundary line, they urged him to avoid hasty measures, to act if possible in concert with the governor of Maryland. When Keith himself returned to town on July 2, he met a chilly reception from the Council. "The proceedings of the Governor, so far as they concern or touch with the Proprietary affairs of this province," Logan minuted, "are judged by the Council not to lie before this board." In other words, the Governor had stepped outside his authority again, had infringed the powers of Logan, Norris, and Hill, the Commissioners of Property.

After this brush, Keith scarcely troubled to call the

Council together, except on Indian affairs. He composed a stinging letter to Hannah Penn. "Mr. Logan," he wrote, "has at last put me under a necessity of differing very widely from him in many things relating to the affairs of your family here." The Secretary, he complained, allowed him no part in the management of Proprietary affairs but "governs with a most absolute sway." He alleged that Logan's management was "very much to the disadvantage and even destruction" of the Penn family's interest and hinted that Logan was lining his own pockets at the family's expense.

The tide of political feeling was unquestionably running against Logan once more. The October elections of 1722 made that clear. Not one of his friends was elected. The Governor urged the new Assembly to meet for business as soon as possible after their fall plowing. Pennsylvania's situation, he told them — and his words sounded ominously in Logan's ears — called loudly "for a perfect harmony and agreement between the Governor and the representatives of the people." It was small consolation for Logan when the Aldermen of Philadelphia chose him Mayor; it meant only that his merchant friends, now in control of the town corporation, still had confidence in him.

His relations with Keith worsened during the Assembly's adjournment. The Governor, reading over Logan's Council minutes, came upon his account of the stormy meeting of April 16, when the Commissioners of Property had questioned his right to order surveys and he had lost his temper. He accused Logan of falsifying the record. Privately, Logan suspected Keith of wanting certain passages expunged because, though accurate, they were "derogatory to himself." It was not long before Logan learned of the charges Keith had made against him in his letter to Hannah Penn. Still he could not bring himself to recommend Keith's dismissal. The Governor might be addicted to "some of the arts of rising at court"; but he was preferable to a stupid, obstinate, conceited creature like Gookin. The important thing was that the Penns should put their own house in order — compose the family squabble over the right of government and thus end the uncertainties out of which Keith was skillfully building himself an independent authority, settle the boundary dispute with Lord Baltimore and prevent a civil war on the frontier, establish their shaky title to the Lower Counties on a firm footing. If no one else could persuade the Penns to pursue their obvious interest, perhaps it was time for Logan himself to go to England again.

But when he heard the language in which the Governor harangued the Assembly on January 1, 1722/23, he decided he could not leave the province. In that speech Keith aligned himself unmistakably with the popular agitators in their war on Logan and the merchant aristocrats. "We all know," he declared, "it is neither the great, the rich, nor the learned that compose the body of any people, and that civil government ought carefully to protect the poor, laborious, and industrious part of mankind in the enjoyment of their just rights and equal liberties and privileges with the rest of their fellow creatures."

To Logan this was the language of the demagogue. He could forecast the Governor's strategy. Knowing that the new Assemblymen were determined to have a paper-money law, Keith would encourage them, take credit for any revival of prosperity that might follow, and thereby entrench himself impregnably with the people — to the inevitable detriment of the Proprietary interest and authority. Logan and his friends must develop a counter-strategy. He himself, unlike his friend Isaac Norris, was not opposed to paper money as such. Pennsylvania's economy was obviously sick and there was much in Francis Rawle's diagnosis and prescription with which he could agree. He persuaded Norris that, rather than opposing the measure, they should use their influence for a sound paper currency, limited in amount, adequately secured, and properly safeguarded against depreciation.

Logan's forecast was accurate. On January 6, 1722/23, the House resolved that "a quantity of paper money, founded on a good scheme, be struck or imprinted." Logan and Norris were ready. The very next day, they requested an opportunity to present their views on "the danger of ill-concerted schemes in so nice and important a case as the regulation or institution of a provincial currency." On January 8 the two men were given a hearing. If paper bills were issued, they said, great care must be used to guard against the natural tendency of such bills to depreciate, "for credit," they added, "has its own laws, as unalterable in themselves as those of gravity are in nature." Furthermore — now they spoke bluntly, making no concession to the popular mood — there must be no favoritism, no special consideration for the poor, "for they have as little merit as any." If the credit of a paper currency was to be maintained, the amount struck must be small — "just sufficient to pass from hand to hand"; it must circulate only for a limited time; and measures must be taken "to force the sinking of it in course and in a just manner."

Two weeks later, Governor Keith gave the Assembly his views in a speech bristling with innuendo. He agreed with the learned merchants that "credit may . . . be compared to the mathematics." But, he added, "by the subtlety of an artist truth or falsehood in either of them is often so darkly wrapped up and involved" that ordinary plain folk — "general [ly] speaking, much the honestest part of mankind" — are too often confused and hoodwinked. He encouraged the Assembly to issue a generous amount of paper money, scouted the danger of depreciation, made barbed remarks about "usurers and sharpers" who "lie at catch for bargains and make a monopoly of trade by engrossing the current money into their hands."

Early in February the House passed a bill to strike fifteen thousand pounds in paper money. Norris might complain of the amount and gloomily prophesy a wild inflation, but Logan was not alarmed. The law was not perfect, but, thanks in part to his insistence, it contained safeguards against depreciation and it would give Pennsylvania a badly needed currency. "If we have no more of it," he observed, "[it] may prove rather useful than injurious to us."

The exchange on paper money did nothing to improve relations between Governor and Secretary. The minutes of the Council meeting of April 16 still rankled in Keith's mind. Once more, in the spring of 1723, he tried to persuade Logan to alter them. This time he used threats. If the minutes were not recast, he would use his authority as Governor to appoint another Clerk and Provincial Secretary. Logan stoutly refused to alter jot or tittle. On May 20 Keith carried out his threats. Somehow he also got possession of the lesser seal of the province, without which the Commissioners of Property could not make land grants. Suddenly Logan found himself stripped of every provincial office except those of judge and Councilor — and the latter was an empty honor since Keith now paid little attention to the Council.

There was nothing, Logan realized, to be done in Pennsylvania now — but much to be done in England. He made his plans to sail in the autumn.

He could not leave without delivering a parting lecture to the people of Pennsylvania. They had heard enough from the legislative forum about their rights and privileges as freemen. He would remind them from the bench (where he sat as Presiding Judge of the Philadelphia County Court of Quarter Sessions) of their duties as subjects. His opportunity came in September 1723, when he delivered the charge to the Grand Jury.

Governments, he told the jurors (and soon everyone could read his charge in print), were of three sorts: monarchy, aristocracy, democracy. Each had its peculiar merits, but each by itself was prone to degenerate into tyranny. It was Great Britain's singular happiness to have a government compounded of all three. The same mixed form prevailed in all the colonies — except Pennsylvania. Her Charter of Privileges contained a radical defect: by withholding full legislative powers from the Council, it denied the province the benefits of an aristocracy.

Still, felicity was possible for the Pennsylvanians if they would settle their political life on the firm foundations of religion, justice, sobriety, industry, frugality, love of wisdom, love of country. It was well for a state, he declared roundly, remembering Keith's attack on the rich and learned, "to abound in wealth and in wealthy persons"; and wisdom and knowledge were obviously the "most useful qualifications" for public office. Turning to the province's current discontents, Judge Logan spoke frankly, bluntly. "Poverty and want of money," he observed, "has of late been the great cry in this place." But let him who complains ask himself "whether he has been as industrious and frugal in the management of his affairs as their circumstances required." Let him ask whether "credit has not hurt him by venturing into debt before he knew how to pay." Let the artisan, the laborer ask whether he has refused to labor "for such wages or pay as the work will deserve."

Here was the real root of Pennsylvania's troubles. Idle, unthrifty men, he declared, will always "repine and grow envious against those who by greater diligence and circumspection have preserved themselves in a more easy and safe condition of life." They will complain of grievances, cry out against the oppression of the poor, "though perhaps no country in the world is more free from it than ours." These malcontents "grow factious and turbulent in the state, are for trying new politics. . . . They are for inventing new and extraordinary measures for their relief and ease, when it is certain that nothing can prove truly effectual to them but a change of their own measures in the exercise of those wholesome and healing virtues I have mentioned, *viz.,* sobriety, industry, and frugality."

A judge on the bench did not, of course, meddle in politics. But the annual elections were only a month away and everyone who read Judge Logan's charge knew how to construe his closing plea that they choose only such men as "upon a mature examination and full persuasion in their consciences" they considered most capable of serving the country "in the best manner and to the best purpose for the good of the whole."

Six weeks later, Logan rode out of Philadelphia to take ship for London, attended by fifty prominent citizens on horseback. It was not a joyous, a triumphant cavalcade. The elections were just over. The people, disregarding Judge Logan's advice, had chosen an Assembly even more "mobbish" than the last. And the new Assembly had shown its teeth by unanimously electing as its Speaker Logan's old enemy, David Lloyd, whom Keith had already elevated to the Chief Justiceship.

Logan's ship was the *London Hope,* heavily laden with

chests of furs from his own warehouses, some, as always, consigned to the Penn trustees to pay off the mortgage on the province. His six weeks' passage, unlike his last one fourteen years before, was uneventful. Once arrived in London, he made his headquarters at the Pennsylvania Coffee House in Birchin Lane, and immediately busied himself disposing of his furs, buying trade goods, and slaking his thirst for books and learned company.

He spent hours in the London bookshops, browsing happily in Bateman's, Innys's, Giles's, Jackson's — pouncing with joy on a new recension of the Church Fathers, a French edition of Pliny, the latest Newtonian treatises on physics and astronomy. Book collecting had become his passion. He was resolved, now that he had the means, to surround himself in his approaching retirement with the best authors, both ancient and modern. His old friend Josiah Martin agreed to keep him supplied with books, and he enlisted the help of another scholar — the Reverend William Reading, "a very retired and sober student," who was keeper of the library of Sion College, an Anglican foundation on London Wall.

He renewed his old acquaintance with the Quaker scientists Fettiplace Bellers and Joseph Williamson, and struck up a new one with Peter Collinson, the botanist, who had a genius for friendship and an especial fondness for Americans. Through these friends he met the celebrated physician and naturalist Sir Hans Sloane and was shown through his famous collections, which would one day form the basis of the British Museum. He met Edmund Halley, Flamsteed's successor as Astronomer Royal, and managed to acquire from Innys, the bookseller, a copy of Halley's unpublished astronomical tables. And one memorable day he spent two hours at the Royal Society's rooms in Crane Court, listening to the discussions of the virtuosi. There he saw the society's venerable president Sir Isaac Newton, "bending so much under the load of years as that with some difficulty he mounted the stairs of the Society's room." It was the crowning experience of Logan's stay in London, for to him Sir Isaac was beyond all question the greatest genius of the age.

All this was sheer pleasure. But Logan had come to England on Proprietary business — to unravel once again the tangled, neglected skein of the Penn family's affairs. Over the still-unsettled boundary problem he labored long and with some success, despite the maddening indifference of Hannah Penn's sons. The young Lord Baltimore, he found to his dismay, was determined to hold out for the true Cape Henlopen as the southern limit of the Lower Counties and the true fortieth parallel as the line between Pennsylvania and Maryland. No agreement was possible on these terms, but perhaps a truce could be worked out in the border warfare pending an acceptable settlement. So on February 17, 1723/24, Logan met with Lord Baltimore, Hannah Penn, and two of the mortgage trustees at the George and Vulture Tavern and had the satisfaction of seeing them sign an agreement that no surveys should be made and no settlers disturbed in the disputed area for a period of eighteen months.

With this breathing space assured, he renewed his efforts to buttress the Penns' case with historical evidence. In Sir Hans Sloane's crowded library in Bloomsbury Square he made an important discovery — an old pamphlet by the second Lord Baltimore with a chart showing the boundaries of his province as he had understood them. The chart was based on Captain John Smith's map of 1624 and it showed the northern boundary of Maryland just where Logan believed it should lie — a few miles above the head of Chesapeake Bay. Here at last was the proof he had been looking for. In May, just before he left England, he wrote out another detailed statement of the case, incorporating the new evidence and proposing a compromise settlement.

Even more important than the boundary was the problem of Sir William Keith. Hannah Penn had finally decided to dismiss him. Her uncle, Simon Clement, urged her to give the executive power to Logan, either by himself or jointly with Norris and Hill. Logan promptly quashed this proposal. Neither the people of Pennsylvania in their present mood nor the authorities in Whitehall, he knew, would accept him as Governor, nor had he any stomach for the office. But where to find a successor to Keith? Not, certainly, in the crowd of incompetent, ne'er-do-well place seekers who haunted the coffeehouses hungering for political plums. Moreover, for all his faults, Keith was intelligent, an efficient administrator, a canny Indian diplomat. Perhaps it was still possible to "new mold either him or his ideas." At least he could be restrained in a strait jacket of strict instructions. Logan persuaded Hannah Penn to take the chance.

Accordingly, she signed a stiff letter of instructions to Governor Keith. The letter was drafted by Simon Clement, but every sentence bore the impress of James Logan's strong mind. It began with a stern warning: if Keith imagined himself no longer accountable to the Penns because of the still-unsettled dispute over the inheritance, the family could easily convince him of his error by removing him. The Governor must understand that the Commissioners of Property were responsible for all Proprietary business; he must assist them with the powers of government when requested, but otherwise refrain from meddling. Furthermore, in matters of state, he must act only by the advice and with the consent of the Council, "for it was never intended that every new

Governor should, with an Assembly annually chosen, proceed to make what new laws they should think proper . . . without any other check." In particular, he was to sign no more paper-money laws, for "the merchants here inveigh very much against them." Finally, he must reinstate Logan as Secretary and Clerk of Council, and restore to him the lesser seal. Armed with this missive, Logan left London late in May, 1724, for Deal, where a ship for Pennsylvania waited.

When he landed in Philadelphia after seven weeks at sea, he found that Sir William had been riding high in his absence. He had signed bills tripling the amount of paper money in circulation. He had so packed the Council with his followers that Norris and Hill found it futile to attend. In the Lower Counties he was even referring to himself openly as the royal governor. Logan promptly held a private conference with him, showed him Hannah Penn's letter, and waited for his reaction. It was immediate and dismaying. The instructions, Keith exploded, were utterly inconsistent, contrary to the constitution, altogether without force. He would pay no attention to them. Logan was startled and chagrined — startled that a deputy governor should be so insubordinate, chagrined that he himself had been so blind as to recommend keeping Keith in office. He reported the Governor's reaction to Hannah Penn and recommended his prompt dismissal as the only "possible remedy . . . to disorders."

Keith also wrote a letter to Hannah Penn. He professed hearty inclinations to obey her lawful commands but declared flatly that her recent instructions were unlawful and therefore not binding. He denounced Logan for "hypocrisy," "conceited craft," and "wild resentment." He raked up once again the old charge that

Logan had falsified the Council minutes. Having dispatched this letter, he made no new move until the fall elections provided him with a fresh majority in the Assembly. Then, unchastened and unrepentant, he stood before the new Assembly and a throng of citizens in the courthouse and delivered a superb harangue that squinted at James Logan in every calculated sentence.

Shrewdly he recalled how harmoniously he had worked with the people's representatives over the past seven years, how together they had pulled the province out of depression. But "acts of benevolence . . . amiable to justice and good nature . . . become hateful," he went on, "to the envious proud man . . . to those who soothe ambition and thirst after power under the conceited pretence of subduing ignorance by their own superior knowledge." It was an open secret that Logan had brought back from England some sort of reproof for the Governor. Keith appealed directly to the Assemblymen for vindication. "Is it a crime," he demanded, "to commiserate the distress of the poor and to provide for their relief? . . . Is it a crime to do equal justice unto all men and to appear boldly in defence of the constitution and liberties of your country?" If these things, he told the legislators, were to be accounted maladministration, "it is high time for you to look to yourselves and endeavor to ward off the blow by modestly asserting your lawful privileges as Englishmen. . . ."

On January 13 Keith laid Hannah Penn's instructions before the House. Although they were plainly marked "secret" and were clearly intended only for his eyes, he announced it was his duty to share them with the people's representatives in order that they might see how basely their charter privileges were "struck at by the pernicious advice and ambition of some private men." The House considered the instructions. The Charter of

Privileges was solemnly read. It was resolved finally that the instructions were "an infringement of the liberties and privileges by charter granted to the people of this province." There was no dissenting voice. No one, Logan observed bitterly, dared vote against "the liberties of the people."

The Assembly now adjourned for two weeks, after carefully locking up its copy of the instructions in the muniment chest. Governor Keith and Speaker Lloyd — Pilate and Herod in firm alliance, Logan called them privately — spent the interval diligently circulating copies of the instructions among the people and collecting signatures to a petition calling on the Assembly to defend the people's rights. Logan used the time to prepare an elaborate historical and constitutional defense of the Council, the instructions, and the Proprietary power for the edification of the Assemblymen.

It was scarcely calculated to allay the popular discontents, this memorial of Logan's. Once more he argued that a council was an indispensable balance wheel — necessary to check errors of judgment by the people's representatives on the one hand, by the executive on the other. "That great man, the first founder of Pennsylvania," he affirmed, had never intended his province to be without so essential an organ. Unable for lack of time in 1701 to add such a provision to the Charter of Privileges, he had established the Council by letters patent and had bound every subsequent governor by instructions to act only with its advice and consent. It required "great dexterity and skill in popular address to persuade men that to use a Council and to lay a Governor under the restrictions of taking their advice is a mark of tyrannical government and that . . . the more power is lodged in one single person the safer will the people be in the enjoyment of their liberties." He offered to submit the whole controversy to "some of the King's learned counsel in the law" and promised on behalf of the Proprietors to bear all the costs and abide by the decision.

The Assembly was overwhelmed and a little confused. It voted to publish all the documents — Hannah Penn's instructions, Keith's reply, Logan's memorial. But this was not enough for Keith. He made it clear that he would not be satisfied till the House went on record officially supporting him against Logan and Hannah Penn. To prove that he was in earnest he withheld his signature from two pending bills until the Assembly should grant his wish. Finally, on February 9, 1725, he got what he wanted. In a formal address the Assembly urged him to "take no notice nor regard, or comply with" any part of the instructions that conflicted with the Charter.

Logan meanwhile had read the printed journal of the Assembly, had seen Keith's letter to Hannah Penn with its charge that he had falsified the minutes. Shaking with rage, the printed sheets in his hand, he stood up at the Council table and complained that he had been slandered. There was a full discussion in which each member tried to recall just what had happened on that April day back in 1722. At length everyone, including Keith himself, agreed that, although there were certain passages in the minutes "arising (as 'tis supposed) from the warmth of the debate" that could well be deleted in deference to the Governor, the substance of Logan's minutes had been accurate.

The charge of dishonesty could not be made to stick. But Keith knew that Logan was vulnerable at another point — his intellectual arrogance, his contempt for the capacities of the plain countryfolk. He made the most of this in a clever answer to Logan's memorial entitled *The Governor's Defence of the Constitution of the Province of Pennsylvania and the Late Honorable Propri-*

etary's Character. Sarcastically he spoke of Logan's "un-fathomable depth of profound knowledge, that contemns the written letter of constitutions . . . [and] discov-ers to us the more sublime intentions and secret or never-before-known views of princes and great men." Shrewdly he pounced on Logan's account of how the Charter of Privileges had been granted, deftly twisted it into a dishonorable effort to represent the Founder as "an arch cunning sophister," who had granted a charter inconsistent with his own principles, expecting to supply its defects "somehow" by unconstitutional means. Now it was Keith, not Logan, who appeared to be Penn's de-fender. Vigorously the Governor pressed his advantage. The Founder, he declared, had never held such a low opinion of the simple Pennsylvania countrymen as to assume that their laws would need to be corrected and amended by Logan and his wealthy, learned friends.

It was a brilliant and devastating rejoinder, and its effect was reinforced by a second pamphlet that was soon in everybody's hands. Entitled simply *A Letter to a Friend* and supposedly addressed to a plain countryman named Roger, it dismissed one by one all the arguments of Logan's memorial and repeated the sly innuendo that Logan's audacity in picturing "that wise and honorable man" William Penn as "a crafty, cunning deceiver" was "foul ingratitude" to a benefactor who had raised him from "the mean drudgery of rod and ferula to lord paramount of a flourishing plantation." The *Letter* was unsigned, but Logan was certain that Sir William had had a hand in it.

As if by prearrangement, David Lloyd now entered the paper war with *A Vindication of the Legislative Power,* an effective lawyer's brief against Logan's claims for the Proprietary prerogative. Lloyd's chief contribu-tion was the novel proposition that a principal, once having delegated his powers to a deputy, could not restrict or instruct the deputy in the exercise of those powers. He reminded the Assemblymen of their old feud with Logan, accused him of plotting to establish the rule of "one person" in Pennsylvania by gaining an unconstitutional veto power for the Council and packing that board with his own friends and followers. As for the notion that good government required a council made up of substantial men, he observed, with an eye to his audience, that in his experience "a mean man of small interest, devoted to the faithful discharge of his trust and duty to the government may do more good to the state than a richer or more learned man who, by his ill temper and aspiring mind, becomes an opposer of the constitution by which he should act."

The Keith-Lloyd strategy was almost flawless. The Governor now stood before the people as the defender not only of their constitutional privileges but of the character of their revered Founder, the Chief Justice as the vindicator of their cherished legislative power. Logan had been made to appear the enemy of all three, an autocrat, bent on substituting arbitrary power and "personal" rule for William Penn's benevolent frame of government.

But even at Keith's moment of triumph there came rumors from England that the young Proprietors were about to assert themselves by removing him at last from office. He professed not to be disturbed; if he were turned out as Governor, he boasted, he would be the next Speaker of the Assembly. And then, he added, "some will be sorry." To Logan the rumors gave promise of welcome relief. He was "quite tired," he wrote John Penn, "with standing the public butt" to all the enemies of the Proprietary family. He was almost ready to wash his hands of the Penns, retire to his plantation in the country, perhaps even take his family back to England. "The restrictions . . . of gratitude and fidelity" had given him "a vast deal of trouble" over the past quarter century. Still he confessed to "a kind of obstinacy in wearing the chain."

He preserved a stoic silence through the summer and early autumn of 1725, comforting himself with his favorite Roman poets who reminded him how the just and honest man, wrapped in his own inviolable virtue, might withstand the fury of ungrateful mobs, the desperate threats of demagogues. But when he learned that David Lloyd was flooding Chester County with copies of his *Vindication* and publicly implying that Logan's silence was an admission of guilt, he hastily prepared a refutation, which he called *The Antidote* — but decided at the last minute to suppress it. Only when he had a letter direct from John Penn, assuring him that a new governor was commissioned and would soon be on his way to Pennsylvania, did he release his pamphlet.

The Antidote was a point-by-point rebuttal of Lloyd's *Vindication*. Indignantly Logan threw back the charges of "abuses and ill treatment of the people." If Lloyd persisted in raking up "those unhappy times to which he too justly applies the word *tragedy*," Logan threatened to entertain the world with the Welshman's role in Pennsylvania's public life ever since that day in 1700 when William Penn had had to remove him by order of the Lord Justices from every office of trust for the crime of lese majesty. He appealed to his readers as Quakers. Was not Lloyd acting in a manner quite contrary to "that lovely spirit of meekness and charity" that became a Friend? He was trying desperately, Logan wrote, "to put the bearskin on me as if I were to be run down in a common hunt."

It would have been better if Logan had obeyed his first impulse and suppressed *The Antidote*. The new governor did not arrive for six months. Meanwhile Keith coaxed the Assembly into sending the Penn family an address defending his administration, and Lloyd's Quaker supporters in Philadelphia had Logan haled once more before the Monthly Meeting to apologize for talebearing and backbiting. Logan made a reluctant acknowledgment, protesting that he had only been defending his own character and that of William Penn against a vicious attack.

Meanwhile the wordy war dragged on. The most effective salvo was an anonymous pamphlet called *The Observator's Trip to America*, which mingled unblushing praise of Keith with coarse ridicule and abuse for Logan and his friends. Though no names were mentioned, everyone could recognize the "mighty schollard" with "an unruly itch to be continually dabbling with other folks' affairs," who carried about him "in his very gait and phiz, such a wounded conceit of his own person, that he cannot condescend to be commonly civil to his betters or equals, and disdains to be at the trouble of showing the least humanity to those below him." Everyone guessed that the unflattering portrait had been painted in the Governor's house.

Keith's intent in these final months was clear — to "put the bearskin" on Logan and drive him from public life. On March 4, 1725/26, at the close of a defiant address to the Assembly, he handed to the Speaker, David Lloyd, a paper entitled "A Farther Vindication of the Rights and Privileges of the People of This Province of Pennsylvania" — written by David Lloyd. In language that was harsh and clear this document indicted Logan as an "evil counsellor," proposed once again that he be impeached and removed from office. But the Assembly temporized, knowing now that Keith's days were numbered. Politely it returned the paper unpublished to the Governor with the suggestion that it be held "ready to defend the constitution upon another attack."

Logan had skillfully laid the groundwork for this rebuff. With a new governor on the way, and victory in sight, he could afford to come down a little from the high ground he had been holding if by doing so he could head off Keith's last desperate efforts to ruin him. A letter which he had written to a Chester County Assemblyman had been diligently circulated among the other members and was now spread upon the record. He had never maintained, the letter declared, "that the Council of this province under the present constitution, is a part of the legislative authority." He had never said that an act passed by the Governor without the Council's concurrence was void. The sole issue was whether the Proprietary could lay his deputy under instructions and whether the deputy could violate such instructions with impunity. This point, he hinted, would soon be decisively settled.

Keith knew he was beaten. At the end of May he summoned the Assembly to the courthouse to hear his valedictory. It was a shameless paean to the glories of his own administration. When the House returned an address which he deemed insufficiently appreciative, he called them back, demanded that they endorse his glowing self-appraisal. The House did nothing.

The new governor, Patrick Gordon, arrived on June 22, 1726. Logan was out of town, "a-haymaking" at his plantation. Gordon declined to display his commission except in the presence of Logan and the Council. The Councilors were summoned in from the country, and there was a little procession to the courthouse, where the new governor was proclaimed. With ill grace Keith turned the seals of the province over to Gordon, who promptly and "in the handsomest manner" delivered the lesser seal to Secretary Logan. Everyone recognized the significance of this little ceremony — an ambitious governor humbled, a contentious tribune of the people silenced, the Proprietary authority restored in full vigor, and a strong man victorious.

I X

Public Affairs: The Stone of Sisyphus

JAMES LOGAN was weary of Proprietary business. He had worn the Penns' halter, been "the public drudge" in Pennsylvania for more than twenty-five years. Victory over Keith, vindication of himself and of the Proprietary cause brought no exhilaration, no sense of triumph. For Logan it meant only more labor — uncongenial, unrequited, unremitting labor. His duties as Provincial Secretary and Clerk of the Council he gladly turned over to a young man named Robert Charles, who came over with the new governor as his secretary. But willy-nilly, Logan still found himself spending three quarters of his time on public affairs, while his own business suffered. A summer-long bout of intermittent fever following on the exertions of the struggle with Keith had "broken" his constitution, drained his vitality. He must devote his failing strength to the support of his family, for he would soon be in his grave. The young Proprietors were old enough to attend to their own affairs; James Logan must now look to his — even if he must leave Pennsylvania, return to Bristol, to do it.

This was the burden of a long letter Logan wrote to John Penn on October 20, 1726, his fifty-second birthday. The fall elections were just over, and once again the Proprietary party had a majority in the Assembly. It had been a hard-fought campaign, preceded by a barrage and counterbarrage of pamphlets. Keith, refusing to admit defeat, was fighting desperately on two fronts: in London, where he had enlisted his old friend ex-Governor Spotswood in an attempt to have himself appointed royal governor of the Lower Counties; in Philadelphia, where he had announced himself a candidate for the Assembly. Ill though he was, Logan had mapped the strategy, directed the literary gunfire, served as field general for the conservative forces.

Andrew Hamilton had been his able lieutenant on the London front. He had gone to England to act as Hannah Penn's counsel in the pending Exchequer suit. There he had picked up two telling documents which he proceeded to publish. The first was a petition from Spotswood to the King on Keith's behalf, reviving the old argument that the Penn family had no valid claim to the Lower Counties; its publication served to remind the planters down the river that the security of their land titles was bound up with the Proprietary cause. The second was a similar petition from five London merchants, which revealed that Keith, having mortgaged his salary to pay his outstanding debts, was looking to the governorship of the Lower Counties to restore his solvency. Hamilton's pamphlet, *The Case of the Heir at Law and Executrix of the Late Proprietor of Pensilvania in Relation to the Removal of Sir William Keith,* was promptly republished in Philadelphia.

This well-aimed shot had brought only a feeble answer. *The Just and Plain Vindication of Sir William Keith* had ostensibly been written by one of the ex-Governor's friends; but too obviously the adulatory language, the unabashed encomium, the patent falsehoods were Keith's own. It was a tactical error and Logan had

made the most of it in a "merry sheet" which he called
*A More Just Vindication of the Honourable Sir William
Keith*. With heavy sarcasm he had professed doubts that
such a fine gentleman as Sir William could possibly have
written so falsely, so shamelessly, so vaingloriously in his
own behalf. To allay anxieties in the Lower Counties he
had also published *The Honest Man's Interest as He
Claims Any Lands in the Counties of New Castle, Kent
or Sussex in Delaware*, urging all honest men for their
own and for justice's sake to support the Penn claims and
thereby frustrate the Keith-Spotswood plot.

On the actual political battlefield Logan had employed
a risky tactic and had won. Bucks County, he knew, was
now safely in the pocket of Jeremiah Langhorne, a
wealthy country squire. Philadelphia — "this factious
town, where the lower rank of people, Sir William's
partisans, are the more numerous" — was, on the other
hand, impossible to capture, for the "leather-apron men,"
the artisans and tradesmen, had a tightly organized
"electing club" which was determined, so Logan understood, "to leave out every man they can suspect of the
least degree of moderation." Everything depended, therefore, on the vote in Chester County. Learning that David
Lloyd was now at outs with Keith, Logan had urged his
friends in Chester to support the Welshman, taking care,
however, to surround him with "men of judgment, men
of peace." The risk would be great, he admitted, "for
there is no real dependence there, nor can the Ethiopian
change his skin." Still, the chance must be taken, for
Lloyd was perhaps the only man who could defeat Keith
in a contest for the speakership.

On election day there had been riots in the Philadelphia market place; the pillory and stocks were burned
down, and the "leather-apron men" had defiantly elected
Sir William Keith. But Logan's strategy had succeeded.

Bucks had returned, as expected, a slate of substantial Quaker farmers, with Squire Langhorne at their head, and Chester had chosen a mixed delegation, with David Lloyd leading the ticket and several of Logan's friends close behind — just enough to swing the balance against Keith. On the first morning of the new Assembly, Logan reported to John Penn, Sir William had ridden into town "with a cavalcade of eighty horse under the noise of many guns firing." For all this show of strength, however, Keith was not even nominated for Speaker, and Lloyd won the office easily. "Now," wrote Logan with satisfaction, "the great Sir William is dwindled down to the low degree of an Assemblyman in common with the other members."

But even with the elections over and Keith "dwindled down" to a mere Assemblyman, Logan was still saddled with public responsibilities. Major Gordon, the new governor, was an old man — "much deeper in years," Logan suspected, than he had represented to the Penns. A veteran of Marlborough's wars, he prided himself on having been "bred to the camp, remote from the refined politics which often serve to perplex mankind." Unhappily, Logan soon concluded, his understanding was "no way above the business he was bred to." Until Keith vacated the Governor's Mansion, Gordon and his family lived with Logan in his house on Second Street. "The people say he is consigned to me," his host complained, "and 'tis certain that he lies in affairs of government almost as a dead weight upon me." The old man had to be tutored "in almost every paper and every transaction." The contrast with Keith — "whose abilities," Logan generously conceded, "were scarce to be equaled in these parts" — was great. Still, there was about the old soldier "an honest plainness, free from art or disguise," that was refreshing after Keith's duplicities.

Affairs of property took as much time as tutoring the Governor. Logan might chafe and complain, yet so long as the boundary dispute was unsettled, the mortgage on the province unpaid, and Hannah Penn dependent on him, he had no choice but to stay in the Proprietary harness. But presently some of the ties began to snap. In the spring of 1727 word came that Hannah Penn was dead at fifty-five, worn out by her arduous passage through a "wilderness of briars and thorns" since her husband's death. A few months later he learned that, after nearly six years of litigation, the Court of Exchequer had finally handed down a decision settling the family dispute in favor of her children. John, Thomas, and Richard Penn were at last the unquestioned Proprietors and Governors of Pennsylvania. Was there any reason now, he demanded, why they should not take up their responsibilities and let him go free? In reply they calmly sent him a power of attorney to receive all debts due the estate since their father's death. Logan exploded with wrath: did they think he was bound to their service "for life, without redemption?"

In January 1727/28 a "surprising providence" befell him which seemed to put his need to retire from public life beyond all argument. Crossing his yard on Second Street, he slipped on the ice, fell heavily on his left hip. At first it seemed a trifle — painful but not serious, a mere bruise that would soon mend. He was carried into his parlor; a bed was set up for him; camphorated wine, hot fomentations and plasters were applied; and he waited for the pain in his upper thigh and groin to subside. But it was seven weeks before he could stir from his bed and seven more before he could struggle upstairs to his chamber. Meanwhile, his left leg hung useless, grew steadily weaker, leaving him "perfectly a cripple." Not for a year did he learn the real nature of his disability. His brother William, a physician in Bristol, finally diagnosed it from Logan's description, after the Philadelphia doctors had confessed themselves baffled. The thighbone was sheared off just below the joint and a callus had grown between the fractured parts so that they could not be united. He was condemned for the rest of his life to hobble about on crutches.

Now Logan's letters to the Penns became more urgent, more plain-spoken than ever. He pleaded with them, he demanded that they release him from his duties, he warned them that their interests would surely founder unless one of them speedily came over to Pennsylvania. His pleas, his demands, his warnings were calmly ignored. Even when word came in the spring of 1729 that, thanks largely to his labors, the mortgage was finally paid off, the trusteeship at an end, there was still no release. Their father had left other debts, the young Proprietors said, and until these too were paid, they could not act for themselves. "I have sometimes thought," Logan groaned to Simon Clement, "of begging leave of thy cousins to die when my time comes, since no other disability . . . will avail to discharge me." He likened his unhappy lot to that of Sisyphus in Hades, for he seemed condemned eternally to roll the Proprietary stone uphill.

The old problems, the old antagonisms arose in new forms. In 1729 trade in the Delaware Valley fell off, specie grew scarce, and a cry went up for new issues of paper money to restore prosperity. Sir William Keith was no longer in Pennsylvania, having slipped out of the province just ahead of his creditors; but his old support- ers, so Logan reported to the Penns, contrived to "blow up the common people both in town and country even to a degree of madness." It was rumored that two hundred countrymen, mostly recent immigrants, armed with clubs, were ready to march on Philadelphia, join the town mob, and force the legislature to order a new emission. Andrew Hamilton rushed through the Assembly an address to the Governor, asking him to enforce the Riot Act, and the uprising fizzled out.

At the height of the excitement a newcomer to Philadelphia, a young printer named Benjamin Franklin, published a pamphlet entitled *A Modest Enquiry into the Nature and Necessity of a Paper Currency*. Trade could not flourish without a medium of exchange, he argued, and since labor, not bullion, was the real source of value, paper currency secured by land would serve the purpose as well as specie; what was it but "coined land"? Though young Franklin associated with the "leather-apron men," Logan could see the force of his argument, for he had long since recognized that paper money had been "of great service to the country." His only concern was to keep the amount within bounds in order to avoid a runaway inflation. So he advised Governor Gordon to accept an emission of thirty thousand pounds under adequate safeguards, and the crisis passed.

It did not pass, however, without further satirical attacks of the sort Logan had become accustomed to during his three decades in Pennsylvania, attacks in which he found himself ridiculed as a pedant and pilloried as an aristocratic tyrant. A pamphlet called *The Triumvirate of Pennsylvania* represented Logan, Hamilton, and Jeremiah Langhorne as plotting in the council room to smother the new issue of paper money at birth. Logan, as "Pedagogus Matematicus," was accused of scheming still to make the Council a provincial House of Lords with a veto power over the democratic Assembly. Hamilton ("Conivator Pedago") was pictured as a grasping attorney eager to profit from the distress of the people by collecting more legal fees. And Squire Langhorne ("Negroso Bullico") appeared as a manipulator of elections, determined to frustrate the paper-money party at the polls now that he and his coconspirators had "secured the whole running cash of the province into [their] bags." The anonymous author of the pamphlet proposed a remonstrance to the King complaining that Pennsylvania groaned "under the yoke of the most tyrannical aristocracy in the world."

There was a measure of truth in the unflattering portrait of Logan. He wore his learning arrogantly and habitually treated political opponents as if they were dunces or errant boys in the schoolroom. Moreover, he unquestionably cherished the aristocratic principle. Pennsylvania's constitution was still seriously defective in his eyes because it made no provision for an upper house from which men like himself — men of wealth and learning — could temper the follies and extravagances of the provincial democracy.

The aristocratic principle, as he understood it, implied duties as well as privileges. He for one had never declined to bear the burden of public service. He could not decline it now, in spite of his disability and his desire to enjoy a dignified leisure at his new country seat on the Germantown road. When David Lloyd's death in 1731 left the Chief Justiceship vacant, he agreed to accept the office in spite of strong misgivings. "To mount a bench on crutches," he wrote his old friend Thomas Story, was painful, "and to pass sentence of death," he added with a touch of Quaker feeling, "gives me a real uneasiness." The Chief Justice's salary — one hundred pounds Pennsylvania currency — was small compensation for the troubles the appointment gave him. Nevertheless, every spring and fall for the next five years he presided over the Supreme Court of the province and territories, supplying his want of formal training in the law by hours of poring over the legal treatises in his library.

Within a few years he was called upon for even more arduous services. Toward the end of 1735 it became apparent that the elderly Governor Gordon was dying. Under the laws of the province, when the governorship was vacant, the executive function devolved on the Council. Logan, as senior member, would be saddled with the burdens of administration. He implored John Penn to commission a new governor speedily, for, he wrote, "I can scarce bear the thought of acting as President at Philadelphia and much less at New Castle. . . ." But the Penns, as usual, did nothing, and when Gordon finally expired in August 1736, Logan reluctantly agreed to serve as temporary chief executive because the two Councilors next in line were, in his opinion, utterly unfit for the office. He was nearly sixty-three, completely crippled in one leg and stiff with rheumatism in the other. The jolting ride over the "frightful" rutted road into Philadelphia was a torment, and the longer journey to the capital of the Lower Counties, whether by land or water, was an exhausting ordeal. The Penns thoughtfully provided him with a four-wheeled chariot to make his trips more comfortable, but they delayed for months before sending over a new governor. It would be nearly two years before Logan could lay down the duties of chief executive.

As President of the Council Logan was almost, but not quite, clothed with the authority of a deputy governor. The law which provided for the interim administration of the province authorized the President and Council to exercise the powers of government "as fully and amply as any Deputy or Lieutenant Governor of this province may, can, or ought to do, legislation excepted." The central issue of Pennsylvania politics over a third of a century was concealed in those inconspicuous words "legislation excepted." A few weeks after Logan assumed his executive duties, a brief passage of arms between the Assembly and the Council showed that the legislators had long memories. It was a polite skirmish, no more than a faint echo of earlier battles, but it reflected the Assembly's continuing distrust of Logan and the Council, its fear of encroachments on its precious monopoly of the lawmaking function.

A new Assembly convened on October 14 in the new, still-unfinished State House on Chestnut Street (the building that would one day be known as Independence Hall). Its members qualified themselves as usual and elected a Speaker — Logan's friend Andrew Hamilton. They then sent messengers to the Council to announce that they were in session and ready to receive any messages the Council might wish to lay before them. The Council promptly replied that it was sitting in the council chamber at President Logan's house on Second Street and was ready "to receive the House of Representatives with their Speaker according to custom." It was clear from the language of its message that the Council was claiming the Governor's traditional right to approve the Assembly's choice of a Speaker. There was "a long debate upon the meaning of the said message" in the State House. To go through this formality, it was argued, would imply that the Council had a rightful share in the legislative process. While the Charter of Privileges stood, no Pennsylvania Assembly would concede that. But the time for fighting over this issue was past.

The Assemblymen trooped down to Logan's house in a body and, after making their position clear, explained that their scruple about presenting their Speaker "did not proceed from any want of respect for the President and Council, for whom the House entertained a very great regard, as well in their public as private capacities." Logan replied for the Council that the presentation of the Speaker had seemed a decent and traditional form, but acknowledged that "perhaps there might be more in the reasons offered by the House than the Board had apprehended." In any case, since "unanimity on all hands ought principally to be studied as most essential to the well-being of government . . . he hoped all endeavors would be used accordingly to cultivate and improve it."

Since President Logan had no power to sign bills into law, there was little reason for the Assembly to meet except to appropriate funds from time to time for the necessary expenses of government. Consequently there was no occasion for the friction that had usually attended Logan's relations with the legislature in the past. But there was plenty of work for the President to do in administering the laws already on the books. In fact in his two years as executive head of the government Logan encountered "such a crowd of difficulties, one heaped upon another," as he had never known before in his long public career. An important but troublesome Indian purchase on the upper Delaware and a sharp crisis in the boundary dispute, followed by an interminable correspondence with the governor of Maryland, occupied him fully, as we shall see in the next chapter. But, in addition, he had to preside regularly at Council meetings, prepare proclamations and reports, sign commissions and warrants, entertain visiting Indian delegations, listen to innumerable petitions from freeholders, consider appeals from condemned criminals, naturalize hundreds of immigrants. His years and his lameness were a handicap, but Pennsylvania had never had a governor so well equipped by talent and experience for administration. When he stepped down from the presidency in 1738, the Assembly gratefully granted him six hundred pounds for his extraordinary expenses on the public's account. But John Penn, whose delay in appointing a governor had kept Logan in office months longer than he had agreed to serve, merely wrote, "As for my part, I have nothing to send you but my hearty acknowledgments for your many good services both to the public and our family."

Logan gladly relinquished his public responsibilities to Governor George Thomas, who finally arrived in June 1738. But after a lifetime of immersion in politics, he could not disengage himself, even in retirement, from public affairs. A quarter century of peace ended in 1739, when England became embroiled with Spain in the War of Jenkins's Ear. Pennsylvania was ordered to furnish four companies of soldiers for an expedition against Cartagena on the old Spanish Main. Governor Thomas tried to extract funds from the Assembly to arm and equip the men and, like every one of his predecessors, was frustrated by the pacifism of the Quaker legislators. Logan's sympathies were with Thomas — until the Governor made a fatal blunder. He promised freedom to all indentured servants who would enlist, and by so doing alienated everyone, Friend or not, who employed a bound servant. Two rising young Quaker politicians, Israel Pemberton, Jr., and Isaac Norris, Jr., came to Logan, boiling with indignation, to discuss the matter. Although Logan did not share their pacifism, he could agree that military necessity was no excuse for impairing the obligation of contracts.

But he was concerned, as always, over the danger of attack from the west. Out there beyond the mountains, in the valley of the Ohio, Pennsylvania's frontier lay as exposed, as defenseless as ever. And so long as the Assembly was controlled by his coreligionists, supported at the polls year after year by Germans who had come to Penn-

sylvania to escape both war and taxes, the frontier, he
knew, would remain undefended. Conrad Weiser, a German whom he had employed on many an Indian mission,
shared his alarm, and Conrad was a man of some weight
and influence in the German community. As the October
elections of 1741 approached, he and Logan hatched a
plan.

Late in September, just before the elections, Philadelphia would be full of Friends from every part of the
Delaware Valley, come to attend Yearly Meeting. Logan
would marshal all his arguments to persuade them that
they should abandon politics, give way to men prepared
to meet force with force. It was unlikely, he knew, that
the Yearly Meeting would accept his views and actually
advise Friends to step down from the seats of power. Still,
his arguments might stir doubts, raise questions, cause
misgivings, induce some Quaker Assemblymen to step
aside voluntarily and some Quaker voters to stay away
from the polls. Meanwhile Weiser, with Logan's help,
would address his countrymen, reminding them of their
obligations to the King and the Proprietors, urging them
to vote for candidates pledged to defense. Weiser's letter,
revised and polished by Logan, came from Benjamin
Franklin's press on September 20, 1741. Two days later,
when Yearly Meeting was in session, young Billy Logan
laid a long communication from his father on the clerk's
table in the great meetinghouse.

Shrewdly conceived, cogently reasoned, carefully
phrased, the letter summed up the philosophy of government James Logan had been maturing for more than
forty years. He wasted no ink in trying to persuade the
Friends to abandon their religious principle against self-
defense, though he did not conceal the fact that he did
not share this conviction. But he could not forbear one
sly dig at the Quaker merchants: "Although they allege

they cannot for conscience-sake bear arms, as being contrary to the peaceable doctrine of Jesus . . . yet, without regard to others of Christ's precepts, full as express, against laying up treasure in this world, and not caring for tomorrow, they are as intent as any others whatever in amassing riches, the great bait and temptation to our enemies to come and plunder the place." The wealthy Philadelphia Friends — the Norrises, Pembertons, Prestons, Hills — had laid themselves wide open to that taunt.

He went straight to his major proposition. "All civil government," he argued, ". . . is founded on force." Hence — he drew the logical conclusion — "Friends as such in the strictness of their principles ought in no manner to engage in it." Even William Penn himself, he pointed out, had found it impossible to reconcile the demands of government with the peaceable principles of his religion; he had resolved, had he stayed in the province, to act only through deputies who had no scruples against using force. Who could speak with more authority on this point than Logan, who had been at Penn's right hand in that almost legendary time, forty years before, when the Proprietor had been in his province? And since the Founder's day the problem had grown even more pressing. Pennsylvania, by reason largely of Quaker diligence and enterprise, had become a great and flourishing country, Philadelphia a wealthy metropolis, nearly equal to Bristol in the volume of its trade. Undefended, province and capital lay exposed, "a tempting bait" to an enemy, inviting attack by land or sea. The danger was real and imminent. On that point too Logan spoke with undoubted authority; no man in the Middle Colonies was in closer touch with the interior, no man had a clearer grasp of international affairs.

Shrewdly he added certain "weighty considerations that may more particularly affect Friends as a people."

Should they persist in their present suicidal course of neglecting or obstructing defensive measures, the King or Parliament might strip them of their power by vacating the charter — and with their political power would go their precious religious privileges. Therefore, he concluded, the Yearly Meeting should advise all Friends "who for conscience-sake cannot join in any law for self-defense [to] decline standing candidates at the ensuing election for representatives."

Logan's appeal had no immediate effect. His letter was referred to a committee, which presently reported that, as it contained "matters of a military and geographical nature," it was not appropriate to be laid before the Yearly Meeting. Robert Strettell, a dissenting committee member, rose on the floor of the Yearly Meeting to protest. The communication came from an old and respected Friend, a man of wide experience, he said; it was sincerely intended for the good of the Society. But another committee member tugged at his coat and said sharply, "Sit thee down, Robert; thou art single in that opinion." And there the matter ended. Weiser's attempt to detach the Germans from the Quaker party was no more successful. Christopher Saur, an influential German printer, promptly issued a counterblast, scouting the danger of a French war, and urging his people not to desert their old friends, the Quakers. When the votes were counted in October 1741, Quaker control of the legislature was still as strong as ever.

Six years later, in the summer of 1747, it seemed as if Logan's fears were finally about to be realized. The War of Jenkins's Ear had become a general conflict, with England and France once more arrayed in arms against each other. Philadelphia heard reports of French and Spanish privateers off Cape Henlopen, of plundered plantations in the Lower Counties, of a hostile fleet making up in the West Indies to attack the Delaware colonies. As usual, the Quaker legislature did nothing. Logan wasted no time now in trying to influence his fellow Friends. Young Benjamin Franklin was effectually arousing the growing non-Quaker population to bypass the Assembly and take the defense of the region into its own hands. In an anonymous pamphlet called *Plain Truth* he set the naked state of the province before the public and appealed for the organization of a voluntary "Association" for defense. Almost overnight, to Logan's great satisfaction, ten companies of "Associators" were under arms in Philadelphia and more than a hundred elsewhere in the province and territories. Though Franklin kept himself discreetly in the background, he was, so Logan wrote Peter Collinson, "the principal mover and very soul of the whole." The old statesman gave him every encouragement and personally subscribed a large sum to the lottery which Franklin set on foot for the purchase of cannon. Though his own son-in-law, John Smith, published an able defense of Quaker pacifism, Logan — too good an imperialist to be a good Quaker — was still convinced that "government without arms is an inconsistency."

That same summer Governor Thomas returned to England. Though Logan was nearly seventy-four, decrepit and unable to travel, the Penns turned almost instinctively to him and asked him to carry on once again as President of the Council. By way of answer he tendered his resignation from the Council after forty-five years of service, and his son William, a more consistent Friend than he had ever been, was chosen in his place. Nine years later, when James Logan was in his grave, his gloomy forebodings at length came true. Fighting flared out on the Pennsylvania frontier, a prelude to the great war that would eventually drive France from the North

American continent. William Penn's "holy experiment" was the first casualty of that war, for the majority of the Quaker legislators, having the cogency of Logan's logic forced on them by events, resigned their seats or refused to stand for re-election, and thereby turned Pennsylvania's government over to men whose religion contained no injunctions against war. Ironically, it was James Logan's son, Councilor William Logan, the one consistent Friend sitting on the Council, who cast the only vote against the declaration of hostilities in 1756.

X

Logan and the Frontier

FOR THE LAST twenty-five years of his life, Logan's eyes were turned anxiously westward. By 1726 a crisis was unmistakably shaping up along the province's frontiers, a crisis compounded of many elements — intercolonial rivalries (especially the still-unsettled boundary dispute with Maryland), domestic political intrigues, the uncertainties and complexities of Indian relations, and the ineluctable advance of white settlement, with the threat of French aggression hovering always in the background. So far Logan's frontier policies had been measurably successful in preserving an uneasy peace in the back country. But he was convinced that only a Penn, a descendant of Onas, or perhaps only the Crown itself, could save the colony from eventual disaster in the West.

No one knew better than James Logan that a fateful change was coming over the Quaker colony. Every summer immigrant ships came up the Delaware, sometimes two or three a week, to disgorge hordes of new settlers — tough, pious, land-hungry Scotch-Irishmen from Logan's own native soil; "morose and warlike" Palatine peasants from the valley of the Rhine. It was a human inundation. "At this rate," Logan wrote John Penn late in 1727, "you will soon have a German colony here, and perhaps such a one as Britain once received from Saxony in the fifth century." Two years later he was writing: "It now looks as if Ireland or the inhabitants of it were to be transplanted hither." People were saying — and with reason, he thought — that "if some speedy method be not taken, they will soon make themselves proprietors of the province."

Hastily the Council improvised a naturalization procedure, requiring a declaration of allegiance. But once the immigrants left Philadelphia, disappeared into the forest to the westward and northwestward, there was no means of controlling them. Wherever they found "a spot of vacant land," Logan reported, they simply squatted "without asking questions." Challenged to show title, the Germans had a simple answer: "The Proprietor invited people to come and settle his country; they are come for that end, and must live." The Ulstermen had an even more provoking response: it was "against the laws of God and nature," they said, "that so much land should lie idle while so many Christians wanted it to labor on and raise their bread." Logan was driven to strong measures; he instructed the sheriffs to pull down and burn the squatters' cabins. But only an act of Parliament, cutting off the flood, he was convinced, could save the province.

For the swelling population was pressing hard against the limits of the lands purchased from the Indians. Already at some points it was spilling over, and the Indians were growing uneasy. Late in the summer of 1727, a message from Captain Civility came to remind Logan pointedly of the government's agreement that no "Christians or white people" should be allowed to settle beyond the Susquehanna. Logan himself had violated the agreement by authorizing one John Hendricks to take up a farmstead on the far side of the river near Keith's old copper mine. He had done it, to be sure, to forestall interlopers from Maryland, and he had insisted that Hendricks go through the form of obtaining the consent of the Shawnee who hunted there. But the barrier was breached, and before long other settlers were filtering across the river. The complaints of the Indians grew louder, especially against the Irish, who, as Logan admitted, were "very rough to them."

There was only one solution — to purchase the lands beyond the Susquehanna from the Six Nations, who claimed them by virtue of their suzerainty over the Pennsylvania tribes. William Penn had long ago tried to buy those lands through Governor Dongan of New York, but that purchase, Logan now realized, was worthless: a new bargain must be struck. But he was powerless to act; only one of the Proprietors could negotiate with the Indians for lands. And in spite of all his entreaties, his appeals to their self-interest and their sense of obligation to the province, they declined to come over and meet the emergency.

The Susquehanna was not the only danger spot. Some fifty miles northwest of Philadelphia on Tulpehocken Creek, a confluent of the upper Schuykill, a colony of Palatines had been living quietly since 1723. Logan knew how they came there. Sir William Keith had invited them to move from New York, had given them their land without a word to the Commissioners of Property.

In June 1728 Sassoonan, the hard-drinking chief sachem of the Schuylkill Delawares, came to town with a troop of lesser chiefs to lodge a belated complaint. Before a vast audience which overflowed the courthouse, the old chief faced James Logan. Beside him sat Thomas Rutter, a renegade Quaker and a former henchman of Keith's.

Bluntly Sassoonan protested that Christians were intruding on his people's lands, their cattle trampling his people's corn. Logan was prepared. Never, he said, had he knowingly departed from William Penn's rule of extinguishing Indian claims before granting land to white settlers. This complaint, he went on, was a political trick to embarrass the government. He brought out a release for lands to the northwest on which Sassoonan and his fellow chiefs had made their marks ten years before. Sassoonan acknowledged that they had released all their lands below the Lehigh Hills. But Tulpehocken, he said, lay beyond the hills. That might be, Logan replied, but he could take no responsibility for the Palatines' being there. "How they came hither he should now make this audience sensible."

Dramatically he unfolded a document he had hastily sent for from among his papers when he had seen Rutter by the old chief's side. It was a petition from the Palatines to Governor Keith, "who of his great goodness permitted them to inhabit upon Tulpahaca Creek," bespeaking his favor with the Commissioners of Property in obtaining a valid title to their lands. The petition, he said, was in the handwriting of the late Governor's secretary, but it bore, especially in its flattering references to "His Excellency," every mark of having been composed by Keith himself. Perhaps — now he addressed the crowd — those who had put the Indians up to complaining of James Logan would go away satisfied. "They had complained, and they were answered." Turning back to the Indians, he urged them not to molest the Tulpehocken settlers, "but wait till such time as that matter could be adjusted" — by one of the sons of Onas.

But still the young Proprietors did not come. And the Western crisis grew steadily graver. On August 4, 1731,

James Logan presented to the Council a matter "of very great importance to the security of this colony." Unrolling a French map of Louisiana published in 1718, he showed the Councilors how Louis XV was boldly reaching eastward, how he was laying claim to lands in the Carolina and Virginia back country and actually presuming to treat western Pennsylvania, up to the very banks of the Susquehanna, as his own. Nor was this a mere paper claim, to be shrugged off as a mapmaker's fantasy. The French were actively cultivating the Shawnee, a restless, homeless people, demoralized by the traders' rum, who had gradually been drifting westward from the Susquehanna into the valley of the upper Ohio. Logan's own traders had told him how the French were plying the Shawnee with presents, providing them with guns, taking their chiefs on visits to Montreal. Solemnly he warned the Councilors "how destructive this attempt of the French, if attended with success, may prove to the English interest on this continent, and how deeply in its consequences it may affect this province." There was one preventive measure the Council could and must take — it must persuade the Iroquois, "who have an absolute authority as well over the Shawnee as all our Indians," to recall and discipline their vassals at once.

The Council agreed to ask Shickellamy, the Iroquois representative in Pennsylvania, to invite the Six Nations to a treaty; it also resolved, as it had often done before, to prevent traders from giving rum to the Indians. Logan knew this was not enough. Somehow, he felt, he must make the government in Whitehall take notice of the threat in the Ohio Valley and realize how precarious its hold on the colonies really was. He spent the autumn of 1731 preparing a documented memorial on the subject for the eyes of the King's First Minister, Sir Robert Walpole himself.

"Of the State of the British Plantations in America," he headed it. He began with certain axioms of mercantilist policy: that Britain's chief rival was France, that her security lay in her naval force, that trade with her American dominions was vital to her strength and prosperity. "It is manifest," he declared, "that if France could possess itself of those dominions and thereby become masters of all their trade, their sugars, tobacco, rice, timber a nd naval stores, they [sic] would soon be an overmatch in naval strength to the rest of Europe, and then be in a position to prescribe laws to the whole." Swiftly he sketched the history of Britain and France in America — the early voyages of Cabot and Verrazano, the French occupation of Quebec and Acadia, the British attempts to dislodge them, La Salle's discovery of the Mississippi, the exorbitant and unjustified French claims to the entire mid-continent. The French, he wrote, "now surround all the British dominions on the main"; more ominous still, they dared to "bring their own claims within a few miles of the head of the great bay of Chesapeake." Obviously their intent was to drive the British into the sea.

What was the relative strength of the two nations in America? In numbers the French were decidedly inferior. Yet they had perhaps two thousand regular troops stationed in the towns and garrisons of Canada and nearly as many *"coureurs de bois,* who are better at an enterprise than so many Indians." Moreover, "the whole country is . . . under one general command which the people obey with such alacrity that in case of any attack they all fly on the first notice to the place of danger as readily as in a garrison on beating or sounding a call." Most important, "they are now masters of almost all the Indians on the Eastern part of the main."

By contrast the British colonies were deplorably weak. "Each of them is a distinct government, wholly independent of each other, pursuing its own interest and subject to no general command." Their fortifications were negligible, their militia ineffective or nonexistent, their Indians few and unreliable. The Iroquois, once a solid bulwark to the westward, had dwindled in numbers and listened to French blandishments. From their recently strengthened fort at Crown Point the French could easily cut the Six Nations off from Albany and "oblige them wholly to depend on Canada." The Shawnee, he feared, were already lost; his traders reported that the white flag of the Bourbons now flew over their wigwams at Chartier's town on the Allegheny, "and the French are . . . building strong houses for them." In a word, the British colonies were in mortal danger.

The remedy was obvious. The one prerequisite for an adequate defense — even the unmilitary William Penn had seen it thirty-five years earlier when he had drawn up a plan for colonial union — was a unified command, a common authority for the continental colonies. Some Englishmen might hesitate to create any such central authority in America, lest it encourage a revolt from the Crown. Logan dismissed that fear. True, the people of New England "by their education and institutions [were] naturally and peculiarly stiff"; Parliament, he suggested, would do well to pass no more laws like the recent one restricting the Yankees' freedom to cut pine trees in the royal forests. Yet so long as "the colonies are treated with tenderness and humanity and not considered as slavishly subservient to the interest of the country they came from," and more especially, so long as French control of Canada presented a common danger, the possibility of rebellion was slight. If there were risks, Britain must be prepared to take them, for there was much at stake: unless the government took speedy action, the nation itself might perish in the ruin of its empire.

He sent a copy of this striking report to a member of Parliament, asked him to lay it before the Prime Minister. But that statesman, he later observed with a trace of bitterness, "was too busily employed another way to mind such trifles." Logan had a poor opinion of Walpole anyway. Having sensed the portentous forces implicit in the geography of North America, he was sure the Prime Minister was mistaken in seeking to build lasting peace on a mere balance of power in Europe. Besides, he was coming to take a fatalistic view of all public men and measures. As he grew older, the follies of ministers, the errors of governments seemed mere incidents in an inscrutable but sinister pattern of destiny. Great disasters, vast revolutions of empire, he thought, were forming in the womb of fate. Ever since 1710 — he had never forgotten the Sacheverell affair and its sequel, the downfall of the Whigs — Britain's statesmen had been perversely wrongheaded, unaccountably prone to error. He could think of only one explanation for their blunders, their blindness, their persistent neglect of America: *"Quos perdere vult Iuppiter prius dementat."* He tried to steel his mind with stoic maxims: "We are all born vassals to fate. . . .By it kingdoms rise and fall; 'tis vain to contend."

For all his fatalism, he still insisted that one of the young Proprietors must come over and solve Pennsylvania's frontier problems. Subtly, shrewdly, he applied financial pressure. He held back a valuable shipment on their account in the autumn of 1729, explaining ominously that "we may have occasion for more than we shall get in case of any commotion." Even if he were empowered to buy land from the Indians on their behalf, he hinted, it would cost three times what a son of William Penn could have it for. These appeals failing, he finally sent James Steel to England to lay before the Proprietors the terrible urgency of the crisis in Pennsylvania. Unless one of them came over, he wrote in what he intended as an ultimatum, "we may expect a war that would run this province in the extremest confusion, none being worse fitted for it." As for himself, he could do nothing more for them; his strength of body and mind were decaying. "After about twenty-seven years rolling this stone, besides two more spent with your father here, I am now writing the last letter that you will ever receive from me as a person invested according to the common notion with a particular trust."

The ultimatum had its effect. In August 1732 Thomas Penn, Hannah Penn's second son, finally came to Pennsylvania. People thronged the streets of Philadelphia to see him, for he was the first member of the Proprietary family to set foot in the province since the brief whirlwind stay of William Penn, Jr., nearly thirty years before. He came just in time, for within a week six chiefs and fifteen braves of the Iroquois Confederacy arrived in town for the expected treaty.

Thomas Penn conducted the negotiations at Governor Gordon's house. Nothing in his brief experience as a Lombard Street cloth merchant had prepared him for such a role, but with Logan at his side to coach him, he handled himself creditably. Conrad Weiser, who had lived with the Mohawks in New York and now had a farm at Tulpehocken, was the interpreter. Through Weiser Thomas Penn reminded the Indians of the chain of friendship his father had forged with them. He promised to make it yet stronger and brighter. Then with blunt candor he put the question which worried Logan so much: "How [do] you stand with your neighbors the French, who were formerly your cruel enemies . . . [and] how [are] all the other nations of Indians to the northward or westward of you . . . affected towards you?" Two days later — Indian treaties were always deliberate, unhurried — the answer came from Hetaquantagechty, a Seneca chief, who spoke for the delegation. After Queen Anne's war, he said, some chiefs of the Six Nations had gone to Montreal and buried the hatchet with the French. But they were still well-disposed towards the English; when they had heard that Frenchmen were in the Ohio country building trading posts and tampering with the Shawnee, they had warned them off, had complained to Montreal. Penn declared himself satisfied with this answer and invited the Indians to join him in "a friendly glass." Hetaquantagechty responded by throwing "a fine painted mantle of dressed otter skins" over the young Proprietor's shoulders.

Next day, in a conference with the six chiefs, Penn, Gordon, and the Councilors pressed a little harder: would the Six Nations give the Shawnee peremptory orders to come back to the Susquehanna? Yes, replied the Indians, if Pennsylvania would call back its traders from the Ohio country and thereby remove a threat to the Iroquois' profitable position as middlemen. Each side agreed to comply with the other's request by the following spring.

So far the negotiations had been in private. To satisfy the people, the final session was held in the great Quaker meetinghouse on High Street before a huge crowd. Again Thomas Penn made the principal speech. He summed up the articles of agreement, promised to keep the road between Philadelphia and the Iroquois towns "clear from every grub, stump, and log, that it may be straight, smooth, and free," announced that Conrad Weiser and Shickellamy would travel that road as official messengers and go-betweens. Thus strengthened and renewed, the chain of friendship, he hoped, would last "so long as the heavens, sun, moon, stars, and the earth shall endure."

The Council had ordered valuable gifts prepared to confirm the treaty — piles of blankets and matchcoats, dozens of kettles, knives, and scissors, a great store of powder, flints, and bullets, three pounds of vermilion, a gross of tobacco pipes. To each sachem Penn personally presented a fine japanned and gilt gun. The Indians responded with their traditional *Yo-ha,* "a harmonious sound peculiar to them," as the clerk described it, "in which those of each nation now present joined alternately."

Outwardly the treaty was a great success for Logan's policy of employing the Six Nations to police Pennsylvania's woods. But doubts had begun to enter his mind: could the Iroquois really control their subject tribes; and were they actually as firm in their British allegiance as they professed to be? As a hedge against the possible failure of his policy, he decided to deal directly with the lesser tribes too. He summoned Sassoonan to his country house and induced him to set his mark to a deed conveying to the Penns all the Delawares' lands on the upper Schuylkill, east and west of Tulpehocken. By this stroke he eliminated a potential source of trouble to the northwest and liquidated the last legacy of mischief from the Keith regime.

Three weeks later, two Shawnee chiefs arrived in town with Peter Chartier, a half-breed trader. Logan called an impromptu council and demanded explanations: why had they recently sent envoys to Canada? The replies were evasive, unsatisfactory, absurdly mendacious. They had gone to Montreal, the Indians said, because the French governor wanted to see them. What had he said to them? That they must "love all their brothers the English"! Thomas Penn urged them to come back to the Susquehanna, offered them a large reservation "for all time to come." They replied that they would be happy to have the lands set aside for them, but "the place where they now are settled suits them much better." In defiance of Onas's wishes and the orders of their Iroquois overlords, the Shawnee remained on the Allegheny. Just as defiantly the Pennsylvania traders remained there too, exchanging rum for furs. Logan's diplomacy, buttressed though it was by the presence of Thomas Penn, had failed to eliminate the potential danger to the province from the west.

The danger from the south, from Maryland, seemed for a while to be checked. Thomas Penn brought with him an agreement, signed in May 1732 by Lord Baltimore, which gave promise of settling the boundary dispute. By the terms of this agreement the lower limit of the territories was to start, as Logan had contended it should, at the more southerly of the two points of land known as Cape Henlopen. The east-west boundary between Pennsylvania and Maryland was to be run from a point fifteen miles south of Philadelphia — another triumph for Logan, even though most of the Nottingham settlements would be thrown into Baltimore's province. The lines were to be run before the middle of December, 1733.

All this was gratifying. Logan was appointed one of the commissioners to arrange for the surveys and actually made a trip down to New Castle to meet the Maryland commissioners, though the weakness of his leg made boat travel painful and dangerous. But it soon became too clear that Lord Baltimore had repented of the pact and had no intention of carrying it out. Seven times the commissioners met; seven times they adjourned in anger and frustration. Sadly Logan came to the conclusion that Baltimore and his deputy, Governor Samuel Ogle, had no object in view but "to spin out the time limited in the agreement without doing anything." There was no recourse for the Penns now but to a Chancery suit with its interminable pleadings and counterpleadings, the wearisome taking of evidence, the maddening delays, the crushing expenses. In June 1736 the Penns filed an exhaustive bill, embodying the fruits of Logan's years of research on the boundary question. The suit was to drag on for a decade and a half.

Within a few weeks after the dispute was submitted to peaceful arbitrament in England, it suddenly erupted into violence on the banks of the Susquehanna, and Logan, who had just taken up his executive duties as President of the Council, found himself with a civil war on his hands. Five days after he took office on Governor Gordon's death, some obscure settlers on the lower Susquehanna scrawled their signatures on a piece of paper and set in motion a train of events that would keep the Pennsylvania frontier in turmoil and the Council in almost continuous session throughout Logan's presidency.

Pressures and counterpressures had been building up for years along the Susquehanna — the steady pressure of settlers, following the rich band of limestone soil southwestward through the Great Valley; the counterpressure of settlers sent up from Maryland to make good that province's land claims; the sullen, passive resistance of the Indians, loath to yield before the glacial advance of the white man. No one understood those pressures better than Logan. He had always known that some kind of eruption was inevitable unless the Penns found means of relieving them by cutting off the stream of immigration, forcing a settlement of the boundary dispute, or purchasing the lands beyond the Susquehanna. None of these problems had been solved. Now Logan must bear the brunt of the long-prepared explosion.

For nearly ten years settlers from Pennsylvania had been crossing the Susquehanna and taking up lands.

Logan knew it; secretly he had connived at it by authorizing Samuel Blunston, a Lancaster County magistrate, to issue temporary land licenses, grants to be
confirmed when the country should be purchased from
the Six Nations. By the autumn of 1736 more than
fifty families — mostly Germans — were living on the far
side of the river.

Just below them, at Conejohela Creek, near John
Wright's ferry, lived Thomas Cresap, a rowdy, pugna-
cious Yorkshireman, prototype of the advance guard of
settlement on many a future frontier. Lord Baltimore had
commissioned him justice of the peace, land agent,
captain of militia, and — so all Pennsylvania believed —
sent him up the Susquehanna to hold this frontier post
against all comers. Reports of Cresap's doings had been
reaching Logan's ears for years — reports that told of his
abusing and antagonizing the Indians, shooting the Pennsylvanians' livestock and threatening to attach their property, conniving at the escape of fugitives from Pennsylvania justice. More than one pitched battle had been
fought around Cresap's cabin; in one of them Cresap
had shot and killed a Pennsylvanian named Knowles
Daunt. For these acts Cresap had come to be known as
"the Maryland monster." If only part of the stories about
him were true, Logan felt, such a "vile fellow" was unfit
to live in any civil government.

In August 1736 Samuel Blunston brought Logan the
latest news from the Susquehanna country. Some Germans from the far side of the river had recently come to
him in great perplexity. The Marylanders had tricked
them, they complained, by telling them the river itself
was the boundary between the two provinces and that
consequently they were living on Lord Baltimore's soil.
In their ignorance and political naïveté they had swal-
lowed this fiction, had sworn allegiance to Baltimore.

Now they realized that they had been imposed upon, and wished to transfer their allegiance back to Pennsylvania. Friend Blunston had advised them to proceed cautiously, openly, and, if possible, in unity, to explain their proceedings fully to the Maryland authorities, and petition the Pennsylvania Council to be taken back under the protection of its laws.

The settlers had followed Blunston's advice. When Governor Ogle of Maryland received their letter complaining of "oppression and ill usage," he promptly notified Logan that he regarded them as factious and mutinous; he was taking "the most proper measures" to reduce them to obedience. There was no doubt about what Ogle considered proper measures. Already a body of armed men was reported marching north "with beat of drum and sound of trumpet" to reinforce Cresap. They arrived at his cabin on September 4, two — some said three — hundred strong, under the command of William Hammond, Sheriff of Baltimore County, armed with carbines, pistols, and cutlasses. At the house of John Wright, Jr., just above Cresap's, Samuel Smith, the High Sheriff of Lancaster County, assembled a counterforce of a hundred and fifty men, mostly unarmed Quakers and nonresistant Mennonites.

For forty-eight hours the two little armies faced each other, while messages were carried back and forth through the woods. Why, demanded Sheriff Smith, were the Marylanders there, disturbing the peace of Pennsylvania? They were there, retorted Sheriff Hammond, to preserve the peace of Maryland. Hammond's men, growing restless for action, presently took two prisoners and plundered some of the Germans' cabins of linen and pewter on the pretense of collecting "public dues." After two days they retired from the field, promising the Germans a temporary remission of taxes if they would return to their Maryland allegiance, but threatening to come back and "turn them out of doors" if they did not.

Logan and the Council were kept informed of every move and countermove. They authorized Sheriff Smith to "be ready with the posse of the county to protect and defend His Majesty's subjects . . . from all insults and outrages." They assured the Germans that Pennsylvania would extend to them the protection of its laws, though it could hardly keep a large garrison permanently stationed across the river to defend them. Having taken these steps, Logan composed a reply to Governor Ogle. Stoutly he denied Ogle's charge that the Pennsylvania authorities were responsible for the Germans' *volte-face*. Firmly he pointed out that the Germans' farms — and by implication Cresap's too — lay miles above the line Lord Baltimore had accepted as the northern limit of his province in the 1732 agreement. The people of Pennsylvania, especially those in the back country, had too much spirit, he declared, to brook any repetition of the recent invasion. "If any mischief ensue on their opposition to your attacks, you cannot but well know who must be accountable for it."

Ogle meanwhile had not been waiting passively. He knew as well as Logan how crucial the Indians were in this backwoods power struggle. Hearing that some Iroquois chiefs were on their way to Philadelphia to sell their trans-Susquehanna lands to Thomas Penn, he sent envoys to intercept them and invite them to Annapolis. Logan got wind of this move and wrote quickly to Conrad Weiser at Tulpehocken: he must hurry over the mountains, meet the Indians at Shamokin on the upper Susquehanna, and invite them to meet Logan for private conversations before the great land treaty. Weiser dutifully followed his orders, reached the Iroquois delegation ahead of the Marylanders, and delivered the invitation.

The party arrived at Logan's country seat on September 27, a hundred and ten men, women, and children, dusty and travel-worn in buckskin and blanket cloth, the old and the lame riding in wagons provided by Thomas Penn, the women carrying burdens, the young chiefs, moccasin-shod, walking with ineffable dignity. For three days James Logan entertained them with food and drink while they rested from their long journey and parleyed in private. On the fourth day they moved to the outskirts of town.

The treaty opened on October 2 in the Great Meetinghouse before a large audience. Logan and Weiser managed the proceedings. After the usual indispensable formalities of kindling the fire, brightening the chain, and clearing the road between Philadelphia and Onondaga, Kanickhungo, the Indians' orator, made an announcement: since the last treaty, the Iroquois had made firm leagues of friendship with all their neighboring tribes, had called home all their people who had been living among the French in Canada. The Council expressed its satisfaction and voted a present of goods worth two hundred pounds.

For a week thereafter Logan and Penn were closeted with the Indians, negotiating the transfer of the Susquehanna lands. Penn agreed to forget the old Dongan purchase and recognize the Iroquois' right to the soil. In return, the Indians consented to sell all their lands lying westward to the setting sun and northward to the Endless Mountains. The treaty was a threefold achievement for Logan — a vindication of his Indian policy, a solution to the problem of Pennsylvania's overflowing population, a victory over Maryland.

But the war on the Susquehanna went on. In November 1736 Logan learned of plans afoot in Maryland to drive the hapless Germans off their farms and replace them with settlers committed to military defense against Pennsylvania. Maryland agents were said to be actually in Pennsylvania, recruiting among the poorer farmers of Chester County. Cresap's cabin was to be the rendezvous and armory for this operation. Sheriff Smith of Lancaster County judged the time ripe for another effort to capture Cresap, against whom he had an old warrrant for the murder of Knowles Daunt. Logan was not privy to the Sheriff's plan, but he understood well that Cresap was "the ringleader of all the mischief done in those parts, the chief engine by which those cruel proceedings were to be carried on in turning the Dutch out of their possessions."

Before daybreak on November 24, Smith and a large armed posse surrounded the crude cabin of squared logs where Cresap, his family, and six confederates were sleeping. In a loud voice he read out the warrant. Then in the name of the Proprietor and people of Pennsylvania he demanded that Cresap surrender. Cresap jumped out of bed, seized his gun with one hand and Hawkins's *Treatise of the Pleas of the Crown* with the other, and, with appropriate references to the law, defied Smith to invade his castle. His legal citations having no visible effect, he turned to oaths, taunted the Sheriff and his men as "damned Scotch-Irish sons of bitches," jeered at the Proprietor and people of Pennsylvania as "damned quaking dogs and rogues." The Sheriff announced that he intended to lay siege to the place and starve its defenders out. Unterrified, Cresap poured himself a glass of rum and drank damnation to himself and his allies if they ever surrendered.

The siege lasted all day. Occasionally a volley of gunfire or oaths from one side or the other broke the silence of the Susquehanna woods. One of Cresap's men climbed out the chimney and gave himself up. Toward nightfall,

the besiegers, growing impatient, set fire to the house.
Only then did Cresap allow his pregnant wife and his
children to evacuate the place. Finally, as the flaming
cabin was about to collapse, he and his men, loaded with
weapons, emerged and made for the river, firing and dis-
carding blunderbuss after blunderbuss as they ran — and
incidentally killing one of their own number. Sheriff
Smith's men quickly closed in, took the five survivors
prisoner. Soon the captives were on their way to Philadelphia in irons. As they came in sight of the Quaker city,
the irrepressible Cresap turned to a bystander and burst
out, "Damn it . . . this is one of the prettiest towns in
Maryland."

The "Maryland monster" safely lodged in Philadelphia
jail, Logan called the Assembly into session, proposed a
joint petition to the Crown praying its intervention to
prevent further acts of violence against Pennsylvanians.
All through the winter and spring of 1737, Logan and
the Council were in almost constant session at his house
on Second Street. Two commissioners came up from
Maryland, bristling with complaints and demands: the
attack on Cresap's house was a barbarous act of aggression on Maryland soil; the innocent victims must be released at once; Sheriff Smith's "incendiaries and murderers" must be delivered up to the Maryland authorities
for trial. Logan and the Council rejected every complaint,
refused every demand. Disorders continued on the Susquehanna frontier, while Logan and Ogle fired letters
back and forth, letters that grew more barbed and full
of recriminations as incident followed incident and tempers wore thin.

It was a full year before peace finally descended in
the Susquehanna country. It came in the form of a Royal
Order-in-Council directing the governments of Pennsylvania and Maryland to put a stop to all "tumults, riots,

or other outrageous disorders" and temporarily forbidding land grants in the disputed area. By the spring of 1738, when Logan turned the executive authority over to Governor Thomas, he could write that the King's order "has given us for the present the blessing of peace."

Not all the immigrants who landed at Philadelphia headed west for the Great Valley and the Susquehanna country. Some pushed northward into the upper part of Bucks County, where two branches of the Delaware came together to form one mighty river. There they found a resentful community of Delaware Indians stubbornly blocking their path, claiming the region as their traditional hunting grounds. Logan knew how desirable the land around the "Forks" was; indeed, he had a heavy investment in an ironworks there and the time would come when he himelf would need more forest land to provide charcoal to feed his hungry furnaces. He had no patience with the claims of the local Indians. In his eyes Nutimus, Lappawinzoe, Tishecunk, the other chiefs of the Forks people were barefaced extortioners, dishonestly demanding payment for lands their fathers and grandfathers had long ago sold to William Penn.

In May 1735 he called them to Penn's old country seat at Pennsbury, showed them a copy of a deed of 1686 which had conveyed to Penn a large tract of land west of the river, extending "back into the woods as far as a man can go in one day and a half." The Indians acknowledged the deed, but insisted that it referred to lands lying below the Forks. Logan was in no mood to haggle. He shifted his attack, tried to discredit Nutimus, whom he considered "a turbulent fellow . . . weak and too often knavish." Everyone knew, he said, that Nutimus had been born in the Jerseys, across the Delaware. By what right, then, did he claim lands west of the river?

Coolly Nutimus retorted by asking how Logan came to have any right in Pennsylvania since he had been born across the great ocean. This insolence was too much. Peremptorily Logan ordered Nutimus and his people out of the Forks. If they did not leave, he threatened, "trees and logs and great rocks and stones" would tumble down into their path to Philadelphia.

Nutimus and his people stayed and the pressure of the white settlers grew steadily more insistent. In the end Logan decided there was only one solution — to overreach the overreachers. First he would cut the ground from under their feet by persuading their overlords, the Iroquois, to renounce all Indian claims to lands along the river. Then he would show Nutimus that the red man was not the only master of chicane.

When the chiefs of the Six Nations stopped at Logan's country house on their way back to western New York from the great treaty of 1736, he had a formal release ready for them to sign with their marks. But the strain of the great treaty, coming on the heels of the Susquehanna crisis, had exhausted him and he collapsed soon after they arrived. ("I just died away for a minute," he wrote Weiser, "and exceedingly frighted my wife, who was with me.") The Indians went on their way, but the faithful Weiser succeeded — not without some difficulty, for the chiefs said they had never claimed lands on the Delaware — in obtaining their marks to the release. He even induced four of them to affirm positively that their cousins the Delawares had no lands left to sell — "and if they offer to sell, they have no good design." Now Logan was ready to deal with the troublemakers at the Forks.

Everything hinged on the old deed of 1686 and the phrase "back into the woods as far as a man can go in one day and a half." The language, like that of most Indian deeds, was vague, but the original intent was fairly clear: Onas was to have had a strip of land lying along the river perhaps twenty or thirty miles in length, but extending no farther north than Tohickon Creek, which entered the Delaware below the Forks. Logan and Thomas Penn saw how the vague phrase gave them their opportunity, how with a little ingenuity they could stretch it to cover the whole area north of the Forks, even to the Kittatinny Mountains. Already, in the summer of 1735, Logan had sent three stout walkers over the ground and satisfied himself that it was possible by hard traveling to cover two or three times the distance the Indians had in mind. On August 25, 1737, he finally induced Nutimus and three other chiefs to sign a document confirming the deed of 1686. Then he and Penn moved swiftly to execute their plan.

They hired three athletic young men as walkers, had trees felled and brush grubbed out to clear a path for them, provided horses to carry provisions and boats to ferry them across streams. At daybreak on September 19, the walk started — not along the Delaware, as the Indians said their grandfathers had intended, but northwestward toward the mountains. Two Indians, who went along as observers, soon dropped behind. "You run," they called out in disgust. "That's not fair; you was to walk." By nightfall the party was well beyond Tohickon Creek, beyond the Forks, and one of the men dropped from exhaustion. A second walker gave up the next morning, unable to keep up the pace over the rough, hilly terrain. But the third persevered until noon of the second day. When he finally fell on the ground, exhausted, he was over the Kittatinny Mountains and twenty miles beyond. He had covered about sixty miles in a day and a half.

The barren wilderness beyond the mountains — worthless to the white man and claimed by the Six Nations anyway — Logan generously left to the Indians. Arbitrar-

ily, he fixed the limit of the purchase at the mountains
and then, just as arbitrarily, ordered the head line run
back to the river, not to the nearest point, but at right
angles to the line of the walk. Since the Delaware makes
a wide sweep to the eastward above the Forks, this stroke
of the pen added thousands of acres to the purchase and
virtually eliminated the remaining hunting grounds of
the Delawares. The offhand, conventional Indian phrase
"as far as a man can go in one day and a half" had been
made to yield some twelve hundred square miles of good
land — "as much ground," Thomas Penn blandly wrote
his brothers in England, "as any person here ever expected." A reservation of ten square miles was set aside
for the Forks Indians in the midst of their ancient hunting grounds. The rest was thrown open to white settlement.

Nutimus and his people complained bitterly. The
walkers, said Lappawinzoe, "should have walked for a
few miles, and then have sat down and smoked a pipe,
and now and then shot a squirrel, and not have kept
upon the run, run all day." Smoldering with hostility,
the Forks Indians remained in their villages, defying
the white authorities to evict them. Logan had unquestionably resorted to sharp practice, but he would not use
force against the Indians. Besides, it was not necessary:
he could always call on the Iroquois to deal with their
recalcitrant subjects.

His opportunity for this and other important business
came in June 1742, when a delegation from the Six
Nations arrived at his country seat to receive payment for
the Susquehanna lands they had sold in 1736. It was the
largest delegation yet, a hundred and eighty-eight men,
women, and children, led by Canasatego, tall, handsome,
barrel-chested, heavy-drinking sachem of the Onondagas.
Presently they were joined by more than forty Pennsyl-

vania Indians, among them the disgruntled Nutimus. As usual, though he was out of public life, Logan fed and sheltered the horde of guests. He did not begrudge the expense — he was twenty pounds out of pocket for their entertainment — for, with a French war looming ominously, he knew it was more essential than ever before to "preserve the Iroquois," keep them safe in the British interest. The Indians, for their part, were disappointed to find their old friend retired from public business and "hid in the bushes." Never within the memory of their oldest men had they conducted an important treaty without him. In spite of his age and infirmities, he agreed to go to Philadelphia, to sit once more by the council fire and assist with the familiar ceremonies — the interminable speeches, the giving and receiving of gifts, the smoking of the feathered calumet.

There was a "handsome dinner" for the chiefs at the Proprietors' house, at which Governor Thomas, with studied casualness, put the momentous question: "I suppose if the French should go to war with us, you'll join them." Canasatego conferred with the other chiefs. Then he acknowledged that the French had been paying assiduous court to them. But they were still faithful, he insisted, to their English allies. This was reassuring. The Council showed its relief by adding three hundred pounds to the agreed price for the Susquehanna lands.

At the conclusion of the treaty, Canasatego, glowing with liquor and good fellowship, did Logan and the Proprietors a special favor. He turned on Nutimus and delivered a thundering philippic, confused and irresponsible, but powerful in its crude, savage rhetoric. The Forks Indians, he said, ought to be "taken by the hair of the head and shaked severely." They had no grounds for complaint about the Walking Purchase. "This land that you claim," he shouted, "is gone through your guts. You have been furnished with clothes and meat and drink by the goods paid you for it, and now you want it again like children as you are." They were not even children, they were women, a conquered and emasculated people, incapable of holding land. "We charge you to remove instantly," he fulminated — to Wyoming or Shamokin, far up the Susquehanna. "Don't deliberate but remove away, and take this belt of wampum."

As Nutimus and his friends slunk out, disgraced and embittered, Canasatego turned again to Governor Thomas and the Council. In quite another tone, he spoke of the love the Iroquois bore James Logan: "He is a wise man and a fast friend to the Indians; and we desire, when his soul goes to God, you may choose in his room just such another person of the same prudence and ability in counseling, and of the same tender disposition and affection for the Indians." It was a touching farewell, a fitting climax to Logan's last Indian treaty. From now on, the burden of Pennsylvania's Indian affairs would have to be borne by others — Governor Thomas, Conrad Weiser, the new Secretary, Richard Peters (whom the Indians already considered "a young Logan"). But their policies would be his policies, carried into a new era.

In 1744 a great treaty was held at Lancaster, attended by representatives from Pennsylvania, Maryland, Virginia, and the Six Nations. It was a crucial treaty, for word had just arrived that the long-expected French war had actually begun. Governor Thomas managed the parley skillfully, induced the Southern provinces to settle their land disputes with the Indians, persuaded the Iroquois to open peace negotiations with their old enemies the Catawbas, extracted from them a promise of continued neutrality during the war. Lancaster marked the triumph of Logan's policies, the climax of Pennsylvania's leadership in Indian affairs. A new star was rising as Logan's set: from now on both the British authorities and the Six Nations would look to a young New York trader named William Johnson for advice and direction. But Logan's eyes were still turned westward and, though he could no longer sit by the council fire or endure the tedious formalities of an Indian treaty, his voice was still heeded by those who had Pennsylvania's Indian policy in charge.

The neutrality of the Iroquois protected Pennsylvania's frontiers during King George's War, which dragged on until 1748. The Peace of Aix-la-Chapelle ended the fighting and ushered in a period of economic conflict. Pennsylvania fur traders and Virginia land speculators, rushing into the Ohio Valley, collided inevitably with the French, who were determined to recapture the fur trade they had lost during the war. It was the prologue to the last act of the Anglo-French struggle for the continent. Logan had watched that struggle for half a century, had grasped its fateful meaning as no one else in the British colonies had done. He did not live to see its denouement on the Plains of Abraham, when Wolfe's victory over Montcalm would settle the destiny of the continent. But he knew, he had always known, what was at stake in the struggle — nothing less than the ultimate triumph of British or French civilization in North America.

Late in 1747 some Indians from the Ohio Valley appeared in Philadelphia — the first official visitors to the Quaker town from any part of the vast Mississippi watershed. Logan recognized at once the significance of their visit. It posed a grave problem in Indian diplomacy, for the Six Nations claimed jurisdiction over the tribes in that region, and to enter upon direct negotiations might undermine the cornerstone on which he had painstakingly built his defensive system. But he saw that a new era was opening, that bold new measures were called for. Conrad Weiser urged direct negotiation and so did George

Croghan, an enterprising Irishman who had a string of trading posts in the Ohio country. After a brief hesitation, Logan added his voice to theirs. Soon Weiser was on his way to Logstown on the Ohio with presents for the Shawnee, the Wyandottes, the expatriate Iroquois, who lived on the southern shores of the Great Lakes. Besides the Council's official gift he carried a private contribution from James Logan — a hundred pounds' worth of gunpowder, lead, flints, and knives. With this un-Quakerly blessing from the man who had managed her Indian relations for half a century, Pennsylvania took the first steps toward opening up the interior of the continent to the British advance.

X I

Stenton

It was in November 1727 that James Logan, weary of the ceaseless strain of politics, the dull routine of trade, decided to "change the town for the country," to retire to his "plantation" on the Germantown road and give himself over to the life he had always coveted for himself, the life of a gentleman and a scholar. After his grievous fall on the ice two months later, retirement seemed as unavoidable as it was inviting, for he considered himself a useless cripple, incapable of any active exertion for himself or the public. "Now," he wrote an acquaintance in Virginia, "if I can make philosophy my mistress for life, it is the only choice in my power that can give me the prospects of any comfort."

He planned to build "a plain, cheap farmer's stone house," but the quarries failed and he was forced to build more expensively of brick. "The model and disposition naturally drew on ornament," he found, and before the house was finished and ready to be occupied in November 1730, it had cost, like most houses, much more than he had expected. Such a spacious and handsome mansion as he had built would inevitably "draw on an expense by visitants," he complained, "which will by no means suit me." It pleased Logan to picture himself as a simple countryman on a Sabine farm, but he deceived no one, not even himself. He was, of course, a provincial grandee of the first rank, and the great house he had built for himself on the Germantown road would stand comparison with Pennsbury, William Penn's beautiful manor on the Delaware, now crumbling into ruin from disuse and neglect. A gentleman's country seat required a name. Logan called it Stenton after his father's birthplace in Scotland.

It was a stately dwelling, three stories high, with a low-pitched, flat-topped hip roof, crowned by two tall, massive chimney stacks. Like the furnishings within, its well-proportioned façade combined Quaker plainness and taste with an undeniable opulence and elegance in the texture of its brickwork, laid in Flemish bond. A parlor and a state dining room flanked the spacious entrance hall, with a smaller family dining room and a bedroom behind. The great room which held Logan's library stretched across the entire front of the house on the second floor. Three bedchambers and a nursery occupied the rest of the second story, and there were four rooms in the garret for the servants. The kitchen, wash house, and cellars stood in the rear.

From his upper windows Logan could see the clear waters of Wingohocking Creek flowing through his estate toward the Delaware. To the westward over the low hills lay the old village of Germantown. A short distance down the road toward Philadelphia was Isaac Norris's country seat, Fairhill. Philadelphia with its crowded streets, its busy market place, its clamorous Assembly chamber was five miles away — far enough so that Logan could feel himself buried in the country, "hid in the bushes," as the Indians said, when they came to visit him. Here at Stenton, surrounded by his books and his family, and waited on by ten servants, black and white, he could at last enjoy the dignified leisure he had always longed for.

Yet he could not entirely withdraw from trade, for, as he wrote Governor Burnet of New York, "unless the merchant exert himself, the scholar will starve." He had two partners now to whom he delegated the management of his routine business affairs. Thomas Lawrence, a New Yorker recently arrived in Philadelphia, supervised the little fleet of vessels in which he carried on his general overseas trade — the ships *Sarah* and *Constantine,* the snow *Rachel,* the brigantine *Little Mary.* His former apprentice, Edward Shippen, handled the details of the fur trade — ordering blankets, guns, and gewgaws from England, haggling with the traders, packing the skins for shipment. But Logan still kept a watchful eye on their accounts.

Just before he moved to Stenton, he had launched an ambitious new enterprise — an iron "plantation" at Durham, far up the Delaware, almost in the shadow of the Lehigh Hills. The land and the furnace were owned in shares by fourteen partners, but Logan's initial investment of one thousand pounds represented a quarter of the total capital, and before long he had sunk almost as much again in the venture. There were already four iron furnaces in the province, but the new one — well capitalized, situated near a good vein of iron, surrounded by six thousand acres of forest for fuel — seemed very promising. Its product, Logan believed, would equal the best Swedish iron. He studied the technique of iron manufacture diligently from the pages of Georg Agricola's *De re metallica,* and supervised the construction of the works from afar.

By the spring of 1728 Durham furnace was in blast. That summer Logan shipped off the first cargo of pig iron from the Delaware Valley, writing confidently to his London agent: "We hope in a few years to be able in this country to supply England with a great part of what they have occasion for." But trouble dogged the Durham enterprise from the start. The shallowness of the upper Delaware made it difficult to float the iron down to Philadelphia. Then there was the problem of transporting the heavy ingots to England. It was out of the question to pay freight charges and the ship captains refused to take them on as ballast, for, "lying in the bottom, [they] would rack any vessel that is fit to cross the ocean to pieces." Moreover, cheap Russian iron was steadily driving the price down in England, and Abraham Darby, the English Quaker ironmaster, was just introducing a revolutionary new method of smelting iron with coke instead of charcoal. By the end of another year, Logan was lamenting that, after laying out about eighteen hundred pounds, he was "likely to be entirely disappointed" in the iron business. The forges and furnace at Durham continued to turn out pig and bar iron for local consumption, but Logan's dream of a steady export trade and a steady source of income for his retirement came to little.

There were other discouragements too. After years of enjoying something like a monopoly of the fur trade, he began to encounter competition from English interlopers, who could bring goods in more cheaply and drive a better bargain with the traders. In 1732 he estimated that he was four thousand pounds poorer than he had been five years earlier. Moreover, much of his accumulated wealth was invested in lands, and when his inveterate melancholy overcame him, he realized that the value of his lands could be wiped out overnight if the French should attack from the rear and drive the British colonists into the sea. As his anxieties grew, he actually began to sell his holdings and invest the proceeds in England. By

September 1733 he had sent nearly one thousand pounds to his brother, the Bristol physician, for investment in English securities. Yet all his fears in the end proved baseless; when he came to make his will in 1749, his estate amounted to eighty-five hundred pounds in cash and bonds and nearly eighteen thousand acres of good Pennsylvania and New Jersey lands. Fifty years in America — fifty years of diligence and prudent management, of native business acumen applied to unusual opportunities — had made the son of Patrick Logan, the impoverished Quaker schoolmaster of Lurgan, a wealthy man.

"Remember . . ." he often told his son Billy, who was twelve when the family moved to Stenton, "I never had anything of value from my parents but my education, and I am willing to give thee as good an one." Unhappily, Billy showed "no genius for learning." Logan had intended to tutor the boy himself, but his wife wisely overruled him. "She thinks," he wrote ruefully to his brother, ". . . that as he wants capacity, so I may patience." So Billy was sent to England to be educated by Alexander Arscott, who was master of the Quaker school in Bristol where Logan himself had once taught. There young William was to perfect his Latin, learn French and enough Greek to read the New Testament, and master arithmetic, at least through long division. In his spare moments the boy was to frequent the Bristol fair, become acquainted with the merchants and the mercantile way of life. From time to time his father would send him a little money to be laid out in "well bought and chosen small cheap cutlery"; these purchases he was to send over to Philadelphia "as a venture on his own account" and the proceeds, if any, would be his for spending money. When Billy came back in 1734, a tall youth of sixteen, his father promptly apprenticed him to Israel Pemberton to learn the mercantile business in the countinghouse of Philadelphia's most successful Quaker merchant.

The two girls, Sally and Hannah, got their education at home; they learned needlework from their mother, while their father supervised their reading in French. Sally, the older, was a girl of quick parts; at the age of nine, to satisfy her father, she had learned the Hebrew alphabet and puzzled out the Thirty-fourth Psalm. Hannah was a tall, grave, comely girl with her mother's pious Quaker disposition: when bolts of gay silks arrived in the ships from London, she invariably passed them by and preferred to have her clothes made of sad-colored stuffs. Jemmy, the baby, was "a hearty child"; but though he knew his ABC's before he was three, he gave little more promise of becoming a scholar than his older brother. Sorrowfully Logan concluded that his children took after their mother: they would have virtue and discretion but little of the wisdom or the learning of this world. He could not but feel that "if they had more of a mixture, it might be of some use to them." It troubled him greatly that he would leave no heirs capable of appreciating the riches of his library.

"Books are my disease," he had once confessed; and now in his retirement at Stenton, in spite of the still-insistent demands of business, politics, and Indian affairs, he gave himself over to his bibliomania. He kept his transatlantic agents busy — Friend Josiah Martin, Librarian William Reading of Sion College, his business correspondents in London, Amsterdam, and Hamburg — searching the book markets of the Old World for rare and scholarly works to line his shelves at Stenton. The difficulties of building a scholar's library at three thousand miles' distance from the sources of books were formidable. One of Logan's ships, returning from England in midwinter, was wrecked and plundered in Delaware Bay. The looters, finding a trunk of "useless Latin books . . . which might only help to discover them," pitched them overboard into the icy waters. A leaf of Matthew Poole's *Synopsis criticorum,* a vast compendium of Biblical commentaries, floated up on the shore in the Lower Counties and was identified by a minister there. It was all Logan saw of that shipment.

But most of the books survived the vicissitudes of the Atlantic, and Logan, sitting in his spacious library at Stenton, devoured them hungrily. He ranged over every field of humane and scientific learning. Already he owned most of the Greek and Roman classics, but he would not be satisfied till he possessed every important scholarly edition.

So he continued his collecting until he had seven editions of Homer, three of Aeschylus, three of Sophocles, six of Horace, four of Virgil, numerous versions of the works of Aristotle and of Plato, to say nothing of the lesser poets, historians, and philosophers. Though he was partial to the ancient thinkers, he did not overlook the moderns, but ordered the works of Ralph Cudworth, the Cambridge Platonist, of Crousaz, the disciple of Descartes, and of Francis Hutcheson, the Scottish philosopher. He had "all the old Greek mathematicians" and he kept abreast of the latest work in the field through the books of John Wallis and French writers like Reynau and Castel. When the third edition of Newton's *Principia* was announced in 1726, he promptly ordered it, though he already owned the first two. (Comparing it with the earlier editions, he was saddened to observe "the prevalency of human passions even in the greatest," for Sir Isaac, he found, had deleted most of the references to "honest Flamsteed," with whom he had had a famous quarrel, as well as a passage in which he had originally given Leibnitz credit along with himself for discovering the differential calculus.)

Oriental studies continued to fascinate him. Eagerly he pressed his correspondents to look out for books in this field — Thomas Hyde's treatise on the religion of ancient Persia, the astronomical tables of Ulug Beg of Samarkand, Ibn Tufail's philosophical romance of *Hai Ibn Yokdan,* the writings of Confucius. Unsatisfied with translations, he sent for grammars and lexicons of Arabic, Syriac, Persian, and tried to puzzle out the originals. Learning that his old friend Robert Hunter, the former governor of New York, had two Arabs living with him in London, he wrote for help; his lexicons, he complained, were useless, for though they were "stored with words relating to . . . camels, palms, etc.," they were utterly wanting in the technical terms he needed to translate his learned books.

Since it was too clear that neither Billy nor young James had inherited his taste for books, Logan began, around 1744, to plan for the future of the library. He could not bear to think that the collection he had assembled with such pains should ever be dispersed. So he decided to give it to the public by creating a trust "to the end that all persons residing in this province, who have been educated in reading and writing, and more especially those who have any knowledge of the Latin tongue, or who study any of the mathematical sciences or medicine . . . may have free admittance . . . with liberty . . . of borrowing any of the . . . books." He designed and erected a small building to house the library after his death on one of his town lots on Sixth Street, near the State House, and set up a modest but adequate endowment to provide for its upkeep and growth. The original deed of trust, drawn up in 1745, did not satisfy him and he later canceled it, intending to execute another. Death prevented him from completing the arrangements, but his heirs faithfully carried out his intent in an instrument establishing the Loganian Library as a public trust. It was a princely gift of over three thousand volumes, a worthy successor of the Bodleian Library at Oxford, a worthy ancestor of the Newberry and Huntington libraries of our own day. No collection of books in colonial America — not at Harvard or Yale, not in Puritan Boston or tidewater Virginia — was better chosen for breadth and catholicity, none was nearly so rich in rare editions of the classics or the great works of the scientific tradition.

Every visitor to Stenton was shown, as a matter of course, through the library. One such visitor was William Black of Virginia, who came to Philadelphia in 1744 with a group of Virginia gentlemen on their way to attend the great Indian council at Lancaster. They stopped at Stenton to pay their respects to Logan and ask his advice about the forthcoming treaty. Hannah Logan poured tea for the guests and Black could hardly take his eyes away from the lovely Quaker girl. But he did deign to pronounce the library "really a very fine collection of books." Its proud owner he found somewhat reserved and crusty, though he had to admit that the old man still had "some remains of a handsome enough person and a complexion beyond his years."

The full, handsome features, the florid complexion which Black noted in his host at the age of seventy are obvious in the portrait which Gustavus Hesselius, the Swedish limner, painted of Logan in his old age. There is also in the portrait a hint of arrogance about the eyes, of imperiousness in the hard lines about the mouth. True, Hesselius's technique as a painter was crude and harsh, but there is no reason to doubt the essential faithfulness of the portrait. For Logan himself admitted that the Swede was "no bad hand" at capturing likenesses, that however unflattering he might be to female sitters, "he generally does justice to the men, especially to their blemishes."

In the middle of February, 1739/40, Logan suffered a stroke, which left his right side partially paralyzed, his one good leg disabled. For a time his memory was affected, and for months he could not hold a pen. But gradually his faculties returned and, except for painful spells of rheumatism which made every movement agony, he maintained tolerable health until after his seventy-fifth birthday. By the end of 1749, however, recurrent fits of palsy began to leave him feeble and helpless. Throughout 1750 the attacks of palsy became more frequent, paralyzing his whole right side, taking away the power of speech. One day late in the year, he called his son-in-law, John Smith, who had married Hannah, to his bedside. The young man heard him mumble something: it seemed that he wanted a letter written to his bookseller, but for what purpose Smith could not make out. Speechless and immobile, the old man lingered on into 1751, long enough to hear the good news that the Lord Chancellor in England had finally handed down a decision in the seventy-year-old boundary dispute between Maryland and Pennsylvania — a decision which upheld most of the claims Logan had labored so hard to establish, and provided the legal basis for Mason and Dixon's famous line of 1763–1767. Toward the end of October, 1751, he became visibly weaker. On the thirty-first, with his family gathered about him, he died "in a very easy manner."

X I I

Quaker Virtuoso

"His life was for the most part a life of business," wrote Benjamin Franklin or one of his associates in the *Pennsylvania Gazette*, "though he had always been passionately fond of study." In his philosophic solitude at Stenton, James Logan embodied an ideal as old as the Renaissance and already on the decline in England — the ideal of the gentleman scholar, the virtuoso. The virtuoso was not a professional scholar austerely dedicated to the single-minded pursuit of truth or a scientist devoted in the spirit of Francis Bacon to the advancement of learning "for benefit and use." He was a gentleman who devoted his leisure time to the enjoyment of learning for its own sake and for the social prestige it brought him. Bacon himself had limned the type with a touch of scorn when he wrote of men who have "entered into a desire of learning and knowledge, sometimes upon a natural curiosity and inquisitive appetite; sometimes to entertain their minds with variety and delight; sometimes for ornament and reputation . . . as if there were sought in knowledge a couch, whereupon to rest a searching and restless spirit; or a terrace, for a wandering and variable mind to walk up and down with a fair prospect; or a tower of state, for a proud mind to raise itself upon."

The seventeenth century had been the heyday of the virtuoso in England. On the level of his own special sensibility he linked the Renaissance with its passion for classical antiquity to the Enlightenment with its curiosity about the natural universe. The early English virtuosi had filled their country houses with collections of ancient coins, medals, and statues; the later ones filled the *Philosophical Transactions* of the Royal Society with descriptions of mechanical marvels and prodigies of nature. But the animating spirit, the special sensibility of the virtuoso was always the same — a quality of passionate wonder at the old, the curious, and the rare. No utilitarian purpose sullied the purity of their delight in their curious studies, and if they sometimes sought to decipher the laws of the natural universe, their motive was the simple fascination of the game and the satisfaction that came from possessing knowledge sealed from the vulgar. Yet it will not do to shrug them off as dilettantes and dabblers: they kept alive a genuine reverence for learning among the leisured classes, and incidentally their passion for collecting and observing served the purposes of more systematic students of nature and art.

Though the virtuoso was no longer in fashion in London — Thomas Shadwell had laughed him out of countenance by creating the ridiculous figure of Sir Nicholas Gimcrack — he could still provide a model for James Logan in provincial Pennsylvania. But Logan was a virtuoso with a difference. He had the wide-ranging curiosity of the type, the indiscriminate enthusiasm for nearly every field of learning, the devotion to knowledge for its own sake without thought of utility, the gentleman's snobbish regard for scholarship as a badge of class distinction; he could even endorse Robert Burton's prescription of study as a remedy for the melancholy to which he was prone. But his virtuosity took a special coloring from his inherited Quakerism. As a Friend, schooled from youth to distrust the imagination, he had no taste for painting and sculpture, normally a consuming passion of the virtuoso. His Quakerism imposed a certain discipline on his scientific curiosity, gave him a respect for the beneficial and practical uses of scientific knowledge. It lent sobriety and a didactic cast to his classical and philosophical studies, and led him finally to a concern with ethics that was quite foreign to the virtuoso temperament. Yet through all his studies, whether in botany or optics, mathematics or astronomy, numismatics or philology, classical literature or moral philosophy, ran the special quality of subjective wonder and delight which was the hallmark of the virtuoso's attitude toward scholarship. Learning might be out of style for gentlemen in England, but in a raw, new provincial society, where the gentleman was on the defensive and traditional culture at a discount, a taste for study could serve an essential purpose both for Logan at Stenton and, as it turned out, for the democratic society by which he was surrounded.

In the autumn of 1726, the rector of Christ Church in Philadelphia lent Logan a copy of William Wollaston's *Religion of Nature Delineated,* a popular work of rational theology which attempted to show how all the truths of orthodox religion could be deduced with geometrical rigor from nature. He was captivated by the book: it was, he thought, "a piece for which one may justly . . . congratulate the age." He was especially delighted with a hint which he found in the section on "Truths Relating to the Deity," where Wollaston had revived the ancient biological theory of preformation — the notion that all living things originated, fully formed, as tiny animalcules, blown about by the wind, lodging first in the male seed, from which they acquired an "earthy substance," then in the female matrix, where they were nourished and brought to birth. Later, in Richard Bradley's *New Improvements of Planting and Gardening,* he came upon the observation that even plants seemed to have their male and female parts. These hints excited his virtuoso's curiosity. He resolved to test them by observation and experiment.

He examined the stalks of Indian corn that grew in his garden on Second Street — he had not yet moved to Stenton — and decided they would make admirable subjects for his experiments. He observed on the tassels "a kind of adventitious dust, scarce belonging to the plant, as if lodged there like dew from the air." Was this "farina" composed of those mysterious animalcules of which Wollaston had written? He stripped the husks from the full-grown ears, examined the kernels. These, he concluded, might "justly be called the *ova* or eggs." To each one, he found, "there adheres a white, fine smooth filament which, excepting that it is hollow, resembles a thread of silk." Was it not likely that these delicate tubes had some part in the reproductive process?

Deliberately, methodically, he planned and carried out his experiments in the spring and summer of 1727. In April he planted several hills of maize in each corner of his garden plot. Early in August, when the plants were full grown, he removed the tassels from one group of stalks, carefully snipped away part or all of the silks from the ears of another group, wrapped the ears of the third group in muslin so that they could receive sunlight and moisture but not the farina from the tassels. The plants on the fourth hillock he left untouched as controls. The results in October were unmistakable. The ears on the detasseled stalks were entirely undeveloped except for one which, as he correctly surmised, had been pollinated by the wind from the opposite side of the garden. The ears from which he had cut away all the silks were also undeveloped and those from which he had removed a part contained ripe kernels in proportion to the number of filaments left untouched. On the muslin-covered ears "not one ripe grain was to be seen." "From these experiments," he concluded, ". . . it is very plain that the farina emitted from the summits of the styles [the tassels] is the true male seed, and absolutely necessary to render the uterus and grain fertile." The hollow, thread-like silks were obviously the tubes by which the "male dust," the life-bearing farina, entered and fertilized the grain.

In great excitement he shared his observations with his scientific friends — Governor Burnet in New York, his brother William, Thomas Goldney, a Quaker botanist of Bristol. In the spring of 1728, in spite of his recent accident, he repeated his experiments and spent hours hobbling about his garden on crutches, peering into the flowers on his pumpkin and cucumber vines, examining peach blossoms and barley heads under a microscope. In every case he found "an apparatus agreeing with the hypothesis." His ardor was only slightly dampened when he learned from Goldney that British botanists had known and accepted the sexual theory ever since Nehemiah Grew had proposed it before the Royal Society a half century earlier. No one had described the mechanics of plant fertilization as precisely as he could now do it — not Camerarius of Tübingen, not Geoffroy of France, not Cotton Mather of Boston, all of whom had experimented with maize. Yet he did not rush into print with his findings, but continued to experiment, to make observations, to read, to speculate on this curious phenomenon. Finally, in 1735, he set his observations down in a letter to Peter Collinson, and they were read at a meeting of the

Royal Society in London. The Fellows, reported a friend of Logan's who was present, were somewhat inattentive during the reading, two thirds of them being engaged in "dissecting a German cabbage and looking for the small fibers in the root of an Indian turnip." Still, they voted to publish an abstract of Logan's experiments in their *Philosophical Transactions,* where they could be read by every botanist in Europe.

Meanwhile, Logan had discovered a young Quaker named John Bartram who shared his scientific interest in plant life. Bartram had a farm at Kingsessing on the Schuylkill, but in his spare time he was a diligent collector of botanical specimens. Already by his own efforts he had acquired an immense practical knowledge of botany though, knowing no Latin, he could not read the learned treatises. Pleased by the young man's extraordinary aptitude, Logan tutored him in Latin, lent him books — Salmon's *Pharmacopoeia,* Culpeper's *English Physician,* Turner's *Herbal* — peered through the microscope with him at the stamens and pistils of the thorny mallow, the convolvus, the succory, the motherwort.

One day in the spring of 1736 he received from Collinson a set of printer's sheets of a remarkable little book by an unknown Swedish naturalist named Linnaeus. The ingenious author, he found, had systematically arranged "all the productions of nature in classes," and the system was based on those very organs whose functions he and Bartram had been studying. He promptly sent off a note to his young collaborator to tell him of the book. "The performance is curious," he wrote, "and at this time worth thy notice." The six sheets which so excited Logan were the first version of Linnaeus's epoch-making *Systema naturae,* a work destined for long life as the basis of botanical classification. Presently Logan had a letter direct from Linnaeus himself — a letter in which, to his surprise, he found his experiments on Indian corn extravagantly praised and himself ranked among the heroes, the demigods of botanical science. The language was so extreme that he felt obliged to demur, to depreciate his attainments as a botanist. But he took the opportunity to recommend young Bartram to Linnaeus's attention. "If God grants him life, and if his narrow circumstances do not hinder," he wrote back in Latin, "you may look for great things from him." It was the beginning of a long and fruitful association between Bartram and the great botanists of Europe. Meanwhile Linnaeus praised the "skill and accuracy" of Logan's experiments to Collinson, urged him to have them published in full. Through the co-operation of J. F. Gronovius, a Dutch botanist, they appeared in Latin at Leyden in 1739 under the title *Experimenta et meletemata de plantarum generatione*. Before many years Logan's lucid account of the experiments he had conducted in his Philadelphia back yard was being cited in botanical treatises published all over Europe.

John Bartram was not the only young scientist to whom Logan gave his patronage. One day, a young workman, a glazier named Thomas Godfrey, appeared at his door, hat in hand, and asked to borrow Sir Isaac Newton's *Principia mathematica*. Logan's surprise at the young man's interest soon gave way to amazement at his comprehension of higher mathematics, his facility at solving abstruse equations. He gave Godfrey the run of his library and helped him with his Latin so that he could read the books more readily. Before long he was asking Godfrey's advice on mathematical problems.

The young man, he found, had an inventive knack. He had devised an improvement on the standard mariner's quadrant — an arrangement of two mirrors by which the image of the sun could be made to coincide with that of the horizon. With this device it was possible to determine latitudes even on the bobbing deck of a small vessel, when an ordinary quadrant was useless. The instrument had already been used successfully, Godfrey told him, on a voyage to the West Indies. Logan asked to see it, kept it for several months, then wrote a description of it to Edmund Halley, the Astronomer Royal.

Not long afterwards he read in the Royal Society's *Philosophical Transactions* an account of an almost identical instrument submitted by John Hadley, a Fellow of the society, who claimed credit for its invention. Logan's suspicions were aroused. Could Hadley have got wind of Godfrey's quadrant? The captain who had taken it to the West Indies admitted having blurted out its secret one night in a Jamaica tavern before a British naval officer who was in the islands on a surveying mission. Logan did his best to vindicate his young friend's claim to priority. He sent inquiries off to Jamaica, he encouraged Godfrey to collect affidavits in Philadelphia, he wrote a second long letter to Halley, whose failure to acknowledge the first increased his suspicions. When Halley went so far as to accuse him before the Royal Society of making false claims for his protégé, Logan enlisted the aid and influence of all his learned acquaintances in London — Josiah Martin, Peter Collinson, John Machin the astronomer, William Jones, the editor of Newton. The last three, being Fellows of the Royal Society, were able to get him and Godfrey a hearing. Their letters were finally read to the society. In the discussion that followed, William Jones contended vigorously that Godfrey deserved credit for the independent invention of the mariner's quadrant, and Machin, after presenting all the affidavits which Godfrey had gathered, observed that if they were not valid proof of his priority, "we must believe that all the people in Pennsylvania combined to impose on the Society, which no reasonable man will do." The letters were published in the *Philosophical Transactions,* but the instrument was destined to come into general use as "Hadley's quadrant."

A few months after this affair, the Royal Society heard another communication from Logan. Addressed to Sir Hans Sloane, now president of the society, and typically heterogeneous in subject matter, it showed how Logan's interests were veering from biology to the mathematical sciences. He started with numismatics, a favorite study of all virtuosi. Some authorities had contended, he said, that there was no authentic example of an ancient Hebrew shekel in existence outside the great collection in the Escurial in Spain. To refute this claim he enclosed one as a gift to the society and made some observations on its Hebrew inscriptions. Then he turned abruptly to botany and defended his account of plant generation against certain theoretical objections. Finally, he presented ingenious hypotheses to explain two optical phenomena that had puzzled and fascinated scientists for centuries — the crooked appearance of lightning and the fact that the sun and moon seem larger near the horizon than at the zenith.

Watching a workman carry a long lath past his window at Stenton, he had noticed how a pane of wavy glass caused a jagged distortion of the image. Why, he asked, might not refraction through the clouds have the same effect on a bolt of celestial fire? The "moon illusion," on the other hand, which nearly every scientist since Ptolemy had attributed to refraction through the atmosphere, could not, he thought, be laid to this cause. He had an alternative psychological explanation. He had often watched the moon rise, huge and round, behind the trees at Stenton. Did not the mind's unconscious comparison of the horizontal moon with the size of the familiar objects close at hand offer a logical explanation? The London virtuosi

listened with interest, voted Logan thanks for his communications, and ordered the last two suggestions published in the *Philosophical Transactions.* They were more
ingenious than important, these little essays, but they reflected the drift of Logan's scientific curiosity in a new
direction — toward the study of light and especially the
phenomenon of refraction.

His next essay in optics was completed on his sixty-
fifth birthday in 1738, just after he had laid down his exhausting duties as President of the Council. He had been
reading Christiaan Huygens's *Dioptrics,* and was full of
admiration for the great Dutch scientist's rules for finding
the foci of lenses. But he was shocked at "the tediousness
as well as the obscurity of the demonstrations." Surely, he
thought, the rules could be proved more simply and directly. He set to work and soon had the proofs worked
out, both by geometrical construction and analysis, with a
clarity that surpassed his expectations. He wrote them out
in Latin and English and sent them to England. Peter
Collinson forwarded them to Leyden, where Huygens had
lived and worked, to be published along with his maize
experiments in 1739.

Logan continued his studies in mathematical optics
with a work on spherical aberration. Again he took
Huygens as a point of departure and sought to prove that
the laws of spherical aberration could be worked out with
absolute mathematical rigor in spite of Huygens's (and
Isaac Newton's) belief that it was impossible. This work
too was published at Leyden in 1741.

In these two treatises Logan established himself as the
most accomplished mathematician in North America. No
other American had his grasp of geometry, of advanced
algebra, of Newton's calculus. Except Godfrey and his old
friend Cadwallader Colden, now in New York, there was
no one with whom he could talk the language of higher

mathematics. But Godfrey, though he possessed a strong native talent, was still an untutored genius with no technical training, and Colden, with whom he resumed relations after a long intermission, had an annoying habit of soaring off into metaphysics and indulging in unverifiable abstractions. Logan found a congenial mind in William Jones, F.R.S., one of Newton's ablest successors, and carried on with him a highly technical correspondence that lasted for years. Probably Logan was never happier than when he was writing to Jones, covering his pages with equations and geometrical constructions, letting his mind roam through the clear, passionless realms of higher mathematics. "For bare speculation only," he wrote Jones, "number and measure appear to me to be the most adequate objects on earth for the human intellect."

He had a special fondness for the Greek mathematicians. Pythagoras, who believed that the essence of all being was number, and Euclid, who had reduced the measurement and properties of space to an axiomatic science, seemed to him the ideal philosophers. He spent hours in his library poring over the great folios which contained their works, studying with admiration the commentaries of the medieval Arab scholars and, with less respect, their modern expositors. The fruits of these studies he summed up in letters to Professor Fabricius of Hamburg. Within a few years he had the pleasure of seeing these letters in print. His comments on Pythagoras were published at Hamburg in 1737, those on Euclid at Amsterdam three years later. The name of James Logan was gradually becoming known in the Atlantic community of scholarship.

He still loved to read the ancient poets and historians, for they seemed to mirror a humanity nobler and wiser than what he saw or knew in his own time. He found pleasure in his retirement in turning ancient works into English for the benefit of his children and neighbors who lacked his facility in the classical tongues.

Many years before, he had started to translate the "Distichs of Cato," a collection of moral saws of uncertain authorship from which schoolboys had learned their Latin for fourteen centuries. Soon after moving to Stenton he completed the translation for his own children. The Latin, being of the simplest, presented no problem, though it was no easy task, he found, "to comprise the sense of two Latin hexameters in twenty syllables in English, with a smooth cadence and tagged with a strong rhyme." Nevertheless, he managed to achieve a pithy simplicity in his couplets:

> Act not thyself what thou art wont to blame;
> When teachers slip themselves, 'tis double shame.

Here and there, however, he felt constrained to add a line of his own to improve his pagan author's morality:

> Him who is kind in words but false in heart,
> In his own coin repay, with art for art;
> [*Yet with unblemished honor act thy part*].

And at the end, feeling a need for a final edifying epigram, he tacked a third line onto the last distich:

> If couched in two flat lines each precept lies,
> Yet brief and strong the sense; let this suffice;
> [*Sound pleases fools, but truth and sense the wise*].

A few years later, for the benefit of his old friend Isaac Norris, who had just passed his sixty-third birthday at Fairhill, down the Philadelphia road, he wrote out a translation of Cicero's noble essay on old age, the *Cato Major*. The Roman's stoic philosophy, his insistence that bodily infirmity need not impair the mind's vitality, his celebration of the serene wisdom, the calm pleasures of old age

— all this appealed to the two old Quaker statesmen. For his own amusement as much as for Norris's edification Logan equipped the text with a set of discursive footnotes in which he drew on all the ancient poets and historians in his library for curious facts about the elderly worthies whom Cicero had cited as examples of a green old age. In his search for intimate facts about Fabius and Hannibal, Cato and Scipio, Diogenes and Pythagoras, there was something of the same romantic feeling for antiquity that drove the virtuosi to collect coins and medals so that they could gaze on the features of ancient heroes. Occasionally there was a welcome seasoning of humor in Logan's footnotes, as when he rendered two lines from Horace thus:

> Old Cato would, 'tis said, with wine
> Make his reverend face to shine.

The translation itself had an easy grace and dignified informality that was worthy of Cicero's own lucid eloquence and far removed from the crabbed and tortuous syntax of Logan's normal English prose.

For Logan as for Cicero old age was a time for philosophizing, for speculating on nature and man and God. Logan the scientist had often marveled at the imperturbable order and regularity of the natural universe, in which every phenomenon was "governed by laws steady and unalterable," every form of life "by certain instincts operating with equal force." Human conduct alone seemed irrational, unpredictable, subject to wild aberrations. Was man "the only exception, the sole contradiction to order in this beautiful system?" It could not be so. There must be a science of morals, a set of rules for finding out right and wrong, as there were rules for calculating the refraction of light rays. In the autumn of 1735, Logan began a treatise on ethics. Taking Wollaston's *Religion of Nature Deline-*

ated as his model, he called his book *The Duties of Man Deduced from Nature.*

All through that winter he read and thought and wrote; he considered all the classic problems of philosophy in turn. Against Hobbes he argued, like a good Quaker, that man was formed not for the bloody warfare of each against all but for the peaceful enjoyment of society. With "Dean Berkeley's notion of all being spirit" he had no patience, and "Malebranche's notion of our seeing all things in God" he dismissed as profitless speculation. Though man's knowledge could never penetrate to the real nature, the metaphysical essence of things — here he followed "the great master of reasoning," John Locke — one could trust the reports of one's senses with respect to their external qualities. Furthermore, man was capable of mathematical understanding — a knowledge of the properties and relations of things, a knowledge "wholly abstracted," not dependent on sensation.

Of this order, Logan suggested, was man's perception of ethical truth. The obligations of morality, he thought, were actually self-evident, "founded on the reason of things," like the axioms of geometry. He accepted the theory of Francis Hutcheson that man possessed a "moral sense," an emotional appreciation of the good — a conception not far removed from the Quakers' Inward Light. Together, he believed the head and the heart could perfect morality: the head deducing ethical principles from natural law, solving the problems of human relations by a kind of moral mathematics; the heart through the passions and affections moving man to love and embrace the good. This co-operation, he concluded, was "the true foundation of all social duties."

The Duties of Man Deduced from Nature was never finished and never published. Logan's own public duties as President of the Council distracted him from philos-

ophy and he found himself unable to take up the thread
again afterwards. But in the spring of 1736 he had drawn
from his manuscript a kind of lay sermon which he
delivered from the bench as Chief Justice. Since it was to
be his last charge to a grand jury, probably — at least so
he thought — his last public utterance as a Pennsylvania
official, it seemed fitting that he should say "something
usefully instructive and edifying to the people." So he
exhorted them to imitate in their actions the order and
regularity of nature, to bring forth "those excellent fruits
that yield the only solid comfort and are the true ornament, the beauty of civil life." He sent a copy of his
charge to his old associate and rival in love, Thomas
Story, now living in England. As a Quaker minister Story
felt obliged to remonstrate with him for leaving out of
his system the transforming influence of the Holy Spirit.
Logan reassured his old friend. He was still a Quaker at
heart. Though he seldom went to meeting, though he had
long since rejected Quaker pacifism, he was still firmly
convinced, he wrote, that "something divine attends mankind," an Inward Light shining through the natural conscience, illuminating and vivifying those remains of the
divine splendor which he found in the breasts of all men,
including the heathen writers he loved so well.

The unfinished philosophical treatise was to have been
the crowning work of Logan's intellectual life. In its
concern with the fundamental issues of human existence it
carried him far beyond the superficial and ornamental
studies of the ordinary gentleman scholar. How seriously
he regarded this work was obvious from the care he took
to submit each chapter for criticism to his learned acquaintances in England — Story, Collinson, Josiah Martin,
William Jones, Sir Hans Sloane. But the most searching
and helpful reactions, he found, were those of the young

Philadelphian Benjamin Franklin. Franklin came to Stenton often to talk with him about matters of mutual interest. He was a little awed by the old gentleman's erudition, but he gave his opinions frankly: he ventured to take exception to Logan's "dilate manner of writing" and was inclined to defend Hobbes's theory of *bellum omnium contra omnes* as being "somewhat nearer the truth" than the Quaker's view "which makes the state of nature a state of love." Logan appreciated the young printer's candor, his quickness, his zeal for knowledge. "Our Benjamin Franklin," he wrote Peter Collinson, "is certainly an extraordinary man, one of singular good judgment, but of equal modesty."

In spite of the disparity in their ages, the incompatibility of their political views, the two men sat for hours in the great library at Stenton, discussing everything under the sun from the language of the ancient Picts and the poetry of Lucretius to the newest discoveries in science and the most recent voyages of arctic exploration. One day Franklin showed Logan some "magic squares" he had made while sitting through the tedious debates in the Assembly — ingenious arrangements of numbers which produced the same sum whether added vertically, horizontally, or diagonally. Logan was impressed, compared them with the classical examples in the works of Stifel and Frénicle, and pronounced them "astonishing." Still more astonishing were the experiments Franklin performed with his Leyden jars and other electrical apparatus. The old man even allowed him to administer electric shock treatments for the palsy of his right side. He read Franklin's essays on the cause of lightning and generously acknowledged that they were correct — "notwithstanding my piece in the *Transactions*."

Conscious that Franklin's energy, his zeal for civic improvement and the diffusion of knowledge were work-

ing a momentous transformation in Philadelphia, giving
the life of the quiet Quaker town a new kind of vitality,
Logan lent his support to nearly every one of the young
man's ventures, both private and public. It was he who,
with Friend Israel Pemberton, gave Franklin his first
large print order in 1731 — six hundred copies of a book
by Alexander Arscott, young William Logan's Quaker
schoolmaster in Bristol. When Franklin saw Logan's translation of the "Distichs of Cato," its "precepts of morality,
contained in such short and easily remembered sentences"
appealed at once to Poor Richard and he begged for
permission to print it. With a gentleman's reticence Logan
consented on condition that his name not appear in the
book. Franklin agreed reluctantly — he knew Logan's
name would give, as he put it, "some advantage to my edition" — and the book appeared in 1735. Nine years later,
he published Logan's translation of Cicero on old age. He
lavished special pains on the composition of this book,
printed it in large, clear type with broad margins, and a
handsome red and black title page. *M. T. Cicero's Cato
Major* in Logan's translation was Franklin's typographical
masterpiece.

In his preface to the *Cato Major* Franklin hailed
Logan's work as "a happy omen that Philadelphia shall
become the seat of the American muses." The Quaker
town might never become the American Helicon, but it
was becoming, before Logan's very eyes, the seat of a
genuine intellectual culture. The moving spirits, the chief
promoters and beneficiaries of this awakening were not
the aristocrats of the countinghouse and the council
chamber but humble artisans and farmers like Godfrey
and Bartram and Franklin, "leather-apron men" who had
once shouted for Keith and paper money, members of
the lower classes whom Logan had once scornfully dismissed as having "as little merit as any." It was some-

thing he had not looked for, this concern for knowledge in the lower ranks of society, but it was real, and he did what he could to encourage it.

In the spring of 1732, Franklin and Godfrey came out to Stenton to unfold a scheme they had devised for a subscription library that would make the best books available to men of small means. They turned naturally to Logan as "a gentleman of universal learning and the best judge of books in these parts" for advice on the selection of titles. When the Library Company of Philadelphia opened in the fall — the first collection of its kind in the American colonies — the directors acknowledged his patronage by passing a rule that no one not a subscriber could take books out, "Mr. James Logan only excepted." In time Franklin would be able to boast that libraries on this model had "improved the general conversation of the Americans, made the common tradesmen and farmers as intelligent as most gentlemen from other countries."

When Franklin and Bartram came to him with a second, more ambitious plan for a society of "virtuosi or ingenious men residing in the several colonies, to be called the American Philosophical Society," and asked leave to place his name at the head of the list, Logan unaccountably discouraged them. Perhaps they broached their scheme at the wrong moment — he had always been crotchety and never more so than in his last years — or perhaps he harbored a grudge against societies of virtuosi because the Royal Society had never made him a Fellow; in any case, the American Philosophical Society was forced, as Bartram put it, to "jog along without him."

But to Franklin's third project — his scheme for an academy, which would become the College of Philadelphia and eventually the University of Pennsylvania — he gave his enthusiastic blessing in 1749. Only recently he had declined a flattering invitation to preside over the trustees of a new college just founded across the river at Princeton in New Jersey. As a Quaker he could hardly approve of an institution controlled by Presbyterian clergymen; old and crippled, he could not attend meetings so far from home; and in any case he suspected that the invitation was merely a lure to attract his library to Princeton. But Franklin's proposal for an undenominational school in Philadelphia was a different matter. He accepted appointment as a trustee and, though for years he had not ventured a furlong's distance from his house, he struggled painfully into his chaise and made the arduous trip into town in 1749 to attend a meeting of the board. He gladly gave Franklin leave to describe the resources of his library as an adjunct to the College and Academy of Philadelphia, and even offered a piece of land next to his library building on Sixth Street in the shadow of the State House to accommodate the college.

The Library Company, the American Philosophical Society, the college — unmistakable signs of cultural maturity. The little Quaker town in the Delaware Valley, where James Logan had landed with William Penn in 1699, where he had lived and struggled and prospered and studied for half a century, was already surpassing every other town in North America in trade and population. And what was more important to Logan, it was on its way to becoming the intellectual capital of provincial America.

A Note on the Sources

No COMPREHENSIVE or even adequate biography of James Logan exists. Neither Wilson Armistead's *Memoirs of James Logan* (London, 1851) nor Irma Jane Cooper's *Life and Public Services of James Logan* (New York, 1921) is very useful; both are sketchy, based on insufficient research, and marred by errors. The only approach to a full-scale treatment is Joseph E. Johnson's Harvard dissertation, "A Statesman of Colonial Pennsylvania: A Study of the Private Life and Public Career of James Logan to the Year 1726." Unfortunately, it covers only the first half of Logan's life in Pennsylvania, and it remains unpublished. I am glad, however, to acknowledge my huge debt to Mr. Johnson's sound and exhaustive scholarship.

A few articles have been written on special phases of Logan's many-sided career. Albright G. Zimmerman's "James Logan, Proprietary Agent," *Pennsylvania Magazine of History and Biography*, LXXVIII (1954), 143–176, deals competently and in detail with his services as William Penn's business representative in America. Evelyn A. Benson's article on "The Earliest Use of the Term 'Conestoga Wagon' " in the *Papers* of the Lancaster County Historical Society, LVII (1953), 109–119, deals with the minor question of his connection with that historic American vehicle. Frederick E. Brasch's "James Logan, a Colonial Mathematical Scholar, and the First Copy of Newton's *Principia* to Arrive in the Colonies," *Proceedings of the American Philosophical Society,* LXXXVI (1942), 3–12, was a pioneer study of Logan as a scientist. A more recent, more nearly complete account of his scientific activities may be found in my article "Philadelphia's First Scientist: James Logan," *Isis,* XLVII (1956), 20–30. I have dealt with another side of his intellectual life in "Quaker Humanist: James Logan as a Classical Scholar," *Pa. Mag. of Hist. and Biog.,* LXXIX (1955), 415–438.

In the almost total absence of a secondary literature, the biographer is obliged to approach Logan through the primary sources — a necessity no biographer should regret. Fortunately, the sources are abundant, almost overwhelmingly so. The Logan Papers at the Historical Society of Pennsylvania are voluminous and they can be supplemented from other collections there, especially the Maria Dickinson Logan Family Letters, the Penn Manuscripts, and the Norris Papers. Additional Logan MSS are in the Quaker Collection of the Haverford College Library, the Friends Historical Library of Swarthmore College, the Library of the American Philosophical Society, the Library of the Society of Friends, Friends House, London, and the Royal Society, Burlington House, London.

Parts of Logan's correspondence have been published. Nearly a century and a half ago, Deborah Norris Logan laboriously copied out several hundred of the letters which passed between Logan and William Penn and added some related correspondence from the family archives at Stenton; this material, further edited by Edward Armstrong, was published in 1870 and 1872 as *The Correspondence of William Penn and James Logan* in the *Memoirs* of the Historical Society of Pennsylvania, Vols. IX–X (Deborah Logan's transcriptions, it should be noted, were not always entirely accurate). A considerable amount of Logan's official correspondence was printed without annotation in the *Pennsylvania Archives,* Second Series, Vol. VII. His correspondence with Thomas Story, carefully annotated by Norman Penney, has been published in Volume XV of the *Bulletin of Friends Historical Association* (Autumn, 1926). His letters to William Jones on scientific matters can be found in Stephen J. Rigaud, ed., *Correspondence of Scientific Men of the Seventeenth Century* (Oxford, 1841).

Since the collecting and reading of books was so important a part of Logan's life, the catalogue of his library is a major source for his intellectual life. There are two catalogues: one in MS, dated ca. 1740, at the Library Company of Philadelphia; the other the printed *Catalogus bibliothecae Loganianae* (Philadelphia, 1760). The books themselves, containing many of Logan's marginalia, are, of course, more revealing than any list. Logan's library, still virtually intact, unlike most other major colonial collections, is now part of the Library Company of Philadelphia. Edwin Wolf, 2nd, has written an urbane and knowledgeable description of it in "The Romance of James Logan's Books," *William and Mary Quarterly,* 3rd Series, XIII (1956), 342–353.

Another important physical survival, which deserves to be better known as a splendid example of early Georgian architecture with a Quaker flavor, is Logan's country house, Stenton, now engulfed by the ugliness of industrial North Philadelphia, but maintained in good repair by the National Society of the Colonial Dames of America.

A bibliography of Logan's published writings would be fairly lengthy. All are important to the biographer or to anyone who would understand Logan; unfortunately all of them are rare. I mention here only the most important; there are full bibliographical references to most of the others in my two articles cited above. Some of Logan's ideas on politics and philosophy appear in his three charges to the grand jury: *The Charge Delivered from the Bench to the Grand Jury* (Philadelphia, 1723), *The Latter Part of the Charge Delivered from the Bench to the Grand Inquest* (Philadelphia, 1733), *The Charge Delivered from the Bench to the Grand Inquest . . .* (Philadelphia, 1736). Benjamin Franklin printed his two translations from the Latin, *Cato's Moral Distichs Englished in Couplets* (Philadelphia, 1735) and *M. T. Cicero's Cato Major, or His Discourse of Old Age* (Philadelphia, 1744). His account of his experiments with Indian corn, *Experimenta et meletemata de plantarum generatione* (Leyden, 1739), was reprinted with an

English translation by Dr. John Fothergill (London, 1747). His 1732 essay "Of the State of the British Plantations in America" is printed with a valuable introduction by Joseph E. Johnson under the title "A Quaker Imperialist's View of the British Colonies in America: 1732" in the *Pa. Mag. of Hist. and Biog.,* LX (1936), 97–130. His earlier (1718) essay on the same subject is in Samuel Hazard, ed., *Register of Pennsylvania,* III (1829), 210–212. His letter to Philadelphia Yearly Meeting in 1741 pointing out the contradictions involved in Quaker participation in government is reprinted in *Pa. Mag. of Hist. and Biog.,* VI (1882), 402–411.

The minutes of the provincial Council for the period of Logan's membership are in *Colonial Records of Pennsylvania,* Vols. II–V; the votes and proceedings of the Assembly for the same period are in *Pennsylvania Archives,* Eighth Series, Vols. I–IV. The records of Philadelphia Monthly Meeting of Friends are at the Department of Records of Philadelphia Yearly Meeting, 302 Arch Street, Philadelphia.

On the general history of Pennsylvania in Logan's time the most useful works are Robert Proud, *History of Pennsylvania* (Philadelphia, 1797–1798), an eighteenth-century compilation; Charles P. Keith, *Chronicles of Pennsylvania . . . 1688–1748* (Philadelphia, 1917), a leisurely and copious narrative; Isaac Sharpless, *A Quaker Experiment in Government* (Philadelphia, 1898), a briefer account, written from a Quaker viewpoint; William R. Shepherd, *History of Proprietary Government in Pennsylvania* (New York, 1896), a meticulous analysis of the dual aspect of the Penn proprietorship — ownership of the soil and the right of government; and Winfred T. Root, *The Relations of Pennsylvania with the British Government, 1696–1765* (Philadelphia, 1912), a careful study of the provincial government in its imperial setting. The best recent discussions of the Indian problem are Julian P. Boyd, "Indian Affairs in Pennsylvania, 1736–1762," in *Indian Treaties Printed by Benjamin Franklin* (Philadelphia, 1938), pp. xix–lxxxviii, and Paul A. W. Wallace, *Conrad Weiser* (Philadelphia, 1945). Both these authorities find Logan guilty of sharp practice in the Walking Purchase, but stress the provocations and tend to acquit him of blame for the alienation of the Delawares, which later brought war to Pennsylvania; for the classic statement of the opposite view, which has been followed by most Quaker historians, see Charles Thomson, *An Enquiry into the Causes of the Alienation of the Delaware and Shawanese Indians* (London, 1759). The fullest account of the long-drawn-out boundary dispute between Maryland and Pennsylvania is E. B. Mathews, "History of the Boundary Dispute . . ." supplemented by E. L. Burchard and E. B. Mathews, "Manuscripts and Publications Relating to the Mason and Dixon Line . . ." in *Report on the Resurvey of the Maryland-Pennsylvania Boundary* (Harrisburg, 1909). An important study for understanding the background of Logan's scholarship is Walter E. Houghton, Jr., "The English Virtuoso in the Seventeenth Century," *Journal of the History of Ideas*, III (1942), 51–73, 190–219. On the social and cultural life of the Quaker mercantile aristocracy see Frederick B. Tolles, *Meeting House and Counting House: The Quaker Merchants of Colonial Philadelphia* (Chapel Hill, 1948); on the broader Philadelphia cultural scene, Carl and Jessica Bridenbaugh, *Rebels and Gentlemen: Philadelphia in the Age of Franklin* (New York, 1942).

Index

James Logan is abbreviated JL.

ACTS OF TRADE AND NAVIGATION, 32
Admiralty Courts, 31, 32
Affirmation question, 35, 59
Agricola, Georg, 188
Aix-la-Chapelle, Treaty of, 184
Albany, New York, 36, 111, 165; traders of, 106, 109; treaty (1722), 112
Anglicans in Pennsylvania, 17, 35, 56
Anne, Queen, 37, 40, 60, 81, 82, 115, 116
Antidote, The, 138, 139
Arscott, Alexander, 190, 212
Assembly of Pennsylvania, 20, 49, 51, 52, 86, 118, 119, 123, 124-126, 133-135, 139-140; JL's relations with, 54-55, 57-75, 151-153
Assheton, Robert, 92
Astronomy, JL's interest in, 84, 94-95

BALTIMORE, LORD. See Calvert
Bartram, John, 201-202, 213
Bellers, Fettiplace, 84, 129
Berkeley, George, 209
Bezaillon, Peter, 89, 107
Biles, William, 60-61, 71

Black, William, 194
Blathwayt, William, 33
Blunston, Samuel, 172, 173
Board of Trade and Plantations, 33, 37, 41, 46, 63, 64, 67, 82, 107-109, 116
Botany, JL's interest in, 198-202, 204
Bradley, Richard, 199
Bristol, England, 9-11, 12, 147, 190, 200
Brooke, Harry, 43
Bucks County, Pennsylvania, 59, 61, 144, 145, 178
Burnet, William, Governor of New York, 109, 111, 188, 200

CALCULUS, JL's knowledge of, 78, 205
Callowhill, Thomas, 30
Calvert, Cecilius, second Lord Baltimore, 130
Calvert, Charles, third Lord Baltimore, 21
Calvert, Charles, fourth Lord Baltimore, 130, 170, 172
Canada, 35, 49, 101, 107, 164, 169, 175

Canasatego, 181, 182-183
Canterbury, ship, 12, 13, 15
Carolinas, 103, 104, 108, 120, 163
Carpenter, Joshua, 27, 119
Carpenter, Samuel, 17, 45, 46, 59, 60
Cartagena, Spanish America, 153
Cartlidge, Edmund, 89
Cartlidge, John, 89, 104
Case of the Heir at Law and Execu-
    trix of the Late Proprietor of
    Pensilvania in Relation to the
    Removal of Sir William Keith,
    The, 143
Catawba Indians, 104, 183
"Cato, Distichs of," 207, 212
Cato Major, 207, 212
Charles, Robert, 142
Charles I, 116
Charles II, 114, 116
Charleston, South Carolina, 89
Charter of Privileges, 51, 52, 55, 66,
    68, 73, 118, 127, 133-134, 136,
    151
Chartier, Peter, 169
Chester County, Pennsylvania, 115,
    140, 144, 145, 176
Church of England. See Anglicans
Cicero on old age, JL's translation
    of, 207-208, 212
Civility, Captain, 102, 104, 160
"Claims of the Proprietors of Mary-
    land and Pennsylvania Stated,
    The," 116
Clarke Hall, 42-43, 67
Classics, JL's love of, 95-96, 192,
    206-208
Clement, Simon, 131, 147
Colden, Cadwallader, 98, 205-206
Collinson, Peter, 129, 157, 201, 202,
    203, 205, 210, 211
Commissioners of Property, 22, 26,
    120-123, 131, 161, 162
Conestoga, Pennsylvania, 45, 90, 104,
    111, 121, 122
Conestoga Indians, 102, 104, 106, 109
Conestoga wagon, 91
Conoy Indians, 104

Constantine, ship, 188
Corn, Indian, JL's experiments on,
    199-202, 204
Cornbury, Lord, Governor of New
    York, 38, 39, 47-48
Council, Provincial, 37, 51, 54, 62,
    63, 64, 67-68, 71, 72, 117, 121,
    122, 131, 132, 135, 150-151, 157,
    160, 163, 169, 175, 182; JL Clerk
    of, 22, 25, 123, 126, 132; JL be-
    comes member of, 36, 41; JL on
    powers of, 72-73, 118, 127, 140
Court of Quarter Sessions, 99
Courts, provincial, controversy over,
    61-63, 65-66
Cresap, Thomas, 172, 173, 176-177
Croghan, George, 184-185
Crowley, Sir Ambrose, 85
Crowley, Judith, 85, 92

DARBY, ABRAHAM, 189
Daunt, Knowles, 172, 176
Delaware. See Lower Counties
Delaware Indians, 101, 104, 161-162,
    169, 178-183
Dickinson, Jonathan, 118, 119
Dolmahoy, ship, 23, 31
Donegal, Pennsylvania, 107
Dongan, Thomas, Governor of New
    York, 161
Dublin, Ireland, 9, 11
Dummer, Jeremiah, 84
Durham iron furnace, 188-189
"Duties of Man Deduced from Na-
    ture, The," 209

EDINBURGH, SCOTLAND, 9
Edmondson, William, 7, 8, 9
Euclid, 206
Evans, John, Deputy Governor, 40-
    41, 42-48, 53, 56, 60-63, 64, 65-66,
    67, 68, 70, 75
Evans, Peter, Sheriff of Philadelphia,
    75
Experimenta et meletemata de
    plantarum generatione, 199-202,
    204, 205

FABRICIUS, JOHANN ALBERTUS, 96-97,
    206
"False alarm" of 1706, 44-45, 60, 70
Farmer, Edward, 101
"Farther Vindication of the Rights
    and Privileges of the People of
    This Province of Pennsylvania,
    A," 139
Five Nations. *See* Iroquois Confed-
    eracy
Flamsteed, John, 84
Ford, Philip, 28
Ford family, 29-30, 48, 61, 73, 78
France in North America, 36, 49,
    103, 106, 107-109, 110, 163-165,
    189
Franklin, Benjamin, 13, 154; defends
    paper money, 148; organizes
    "Association" for defense, 157;
    JL's relations with, 211-214
French, John, Sheriff of New Castle
    County, 44
French and Indian War, 157-158
Fur trade, 25, 89-91, 92, 108, 188,
    189

GERMAN IMMIGRANTS, 106, 153, 159,
    160, 161-162, 172,173, 175
Godfrey, Thomas, 202-204, 205, 213
Goldney, Thomas, 200
Gookin, Charles, Deputy Governor,
    48, 49, 71, 73, 75, 100, 104, 117
Gordon, Patrick, Deputy Governor,
    140-141, 145, 148, 150, 168
*Governor's Defence of the Constitu-
    tion of the Province of Penn-
    sylvania and the Late Honor-
    able Proprietary's Character,
    The,* 135-136
Grew, Nehemiah, 200
Gronovius, Johann Friedrich, 202

HADLEY, JOHN, 203
Hadley's quadrant, 204
Halley, Edmund, 129, 203

Hamilton, Andrew, Deputy Gover-
    nor, 31, 34, 35, 36, 37, 53
Hamilton, Andrew, lawyer, 117, 143,
    148, 151
Hammond, William, Sheriff of Balti-
    more County, 173
Harley, Robert, Earl of Oxford, 114
Harris, John, 89
Hendricks, John, 160
Henlopen, Cape, 115, 116, 130, 156,
    170
Hesselius, Gustavus, 194-195
Hetaquantagechty, 168
Hill, Richard, 17, 46, 47, 59, 60, 75,
    86, 118, 119, 121, 122, 131, 132
Hobbes, Thomas, 209, 211
*Honest Man's Interest as He Claims
    Any Lands in the Counties of
    New Castle, Kent or Sussex in
    Delaware, The,* 144
Hope Galley, 75, 76, 79, 80, 81
Hunter, Robert, Governor of New
    York and New Jersey, 97-99,
    193
Hutcheson, Francis, 209
Huygens, Christiaan, 205

IMMIGRATION TO PENNSYLVANIA, 159-
    160
Indian treaties, Whitemarsh (1712),
    100-102; Conestoga (1717), 104-
    105; Conestoga (1720), 109; Co-
    nestoga (1721), 111; Albany
    (1722), 111; Philadelphia (1732),
    167; Philadelphia (1736), 175,
    179; Philadelphia (1742), 181-
    182; Lancaster (1744), 183; Logs-
    town (1748), 185
Indians, JL's relations with, 22-23,
    60, 90, 100-112, 160-162, 167-170,
    174-175, 178-185
Ireland, Quakerism in, 7-8
Iron works, JL invests in, 188-189
Iroquois Confederacy, 36, 101-102,
    103, 105, 106, 107-108, 110, 111,
    161, 163, 165, 167-169, 172, 174,
    179, 180, 181-183, 184

JAMAICA, 11, 203
James II, 8, 9, 62, 114, 116
Johnson, William, 184
Jones, William, 203, 206, 210
*Just and Plain Vindication of Sir
William Keith, The,* 143

KANICKHUNGO, 175
Keith, Sir William, Governor of
Pennsylvania, 104-105, 107, 109,
111-112, 143, 145, 147, 161, 162,
169; JL's struggle with, 117-
118, 121-126, 131-140
King George's War, 156-157, 183,
184

LANCASTER, treaty of (1744), 183
Langhorne, Jeremiah, 144, 145, 148-
149
Languages, JL's knowledge of, 8, 10,
84, 95, 98, 193
Lappawinzoe, 178, 181
Lawrence, Thomas, 188
Lenni Lenape. *See* Delaware Indians
Le Tort, James, 89
Letter to a Friend, A, 136
Lewes, Delaware, 43, 44, 49, 72, 115
Leybourn, William, 10
Light Within (Quaker doctrine), 3,
209, 210
Lightning, 204, 211
Linnaeus, Carolus, 201-202
Lisbon, Portugal, 79-81; trade with,
30, 79, 92
Little Mary, ship, 188
Lloyd, David, 32-33, 60, 144-145; JL's
struggles with, 34-35, 53-59, 61-
70, 72-75, 128, 134, 136-137, 138-
139; Chief Justice, 128, 149
Lloyd, Sampson, 85
Locke, John, 209
Logan, Hannah, JL's daughter, 99,
191, 194, 195
Logan, Isabel Hume, JL's mother, 7
Logan, James
    PERSONAL HISTORY, birth and early
    life in Ireland, 7-9; in Bristol,

9-11; comes to America with
William Penn, 12-14; disci-
plined by Philadelphia Monthly
Meeting, 28, 77, 139; life at
Clarke Hall, 42-43; unsuccessful
courtship of Anne Shippen, 76-
77; in Lisbon, 80-81; in England
(1710-1711), 81-87; unsuccessful
courtship of Judith Crowley, 84-
85, 92; decides to spend life in
America, 85; marriage, 93-94;
buys farm on Germantown
road, 94; friendship with Governor Hunter, 97-99; friendship
with Colden, 98; in England
(1723-1724), 129-132; crippled
by a fall, 146-147; friendship
with Franklin, 157, 211-214;
builds Stenton, 186-188; education of children, 190-191; last
illness and death, 195; friendship with John Bartram, 201-
202; friendship with Thomas
Godfrey, 202-204, 205-206; pa-
tron of Library Company of
Philadelphia, 213; trustee of
College of Philadelphia, 213-214
    BUSINESS CAREER, early ventures,
    9, 11; invests in lands, 86-87; fur
    trade, 89-91, 92, 188, 189; iron
    works, 188-189; investments in
    English securities, 189-190; es-
    tate of, 190
    PUBLIC LIFE, Proprietary agent,
    15-30, 91-92; Clerk of the Coun-
    cil, 22, 25; Receiver-General, 22;
    Commissioner of Property, 22,
    26, 120-121; manager of Penn-
    sylvania's Indian relations, 22-
    23, 60, 90, 100-107, 109-112, 160-
    162, 166-170, 174-175, 178-185;
    defends Proprietary authority
    against Crown, 31-35, 36-37, 38-
    41; becomes member of Council,
    36, 41; relations with William
    Penn, Jr., 41-43, 56-57; diffi-
    culties with Governor Evans, 43-

48, 60-61; relations with Governor Gookin, 48-49, 71; conflict with David Lloyd and the Assembly, 53-59, 61-75; and "good Assembly" of 1705-1706, 59-60; charges of Assembly against, 63-64, 66-70, 72; answers Assembly's charges, 64, 67, 69, 72-73, 74; Presiding Judge of Court of Quarter Sessions, 99, 127; prepares Pennsylvania's case in boundary dispute with Maryland, 115-117, 130-131, 195; conflict with Governor Keith, 117-128, 131-141, 143-145; relations with Governor Gordon, 145; Chief Justice, 149-150, 210; President of Council, 150-153, 171-183; resigns from Council, 157; Pennsylvania commissioner in boundary dispute, 170

SCHOLARLY INTERESTS, astronomy, 84, 94-95, 129; botany, 198-202, 204; classics, 95-97, 192, 206-208; languages, 8, 10, 84, 95, 98, 193; mathematics, 10, 78-79, 192, 205-206, 211; numismatics, 204; optics, 204-205; Oriental studies, 95, 193; philosophy, 192, 208-211; Scandinavian studies, 95

LIBRARY, 10, 11, 129, 187, 191-194

WRITINGS, charges to grand jury, 99, 127-128, 210; memorandum to Board of Trade on the French in the interior, 107-109; "The Claims of the Proprietors of Maryland and Pennsylvania Stated," 116; *The Antidote*, 138-139; *A More Just Vindication of the Honourable Sir William Keith*, 144; *The Honest Man's Interest as He Claims Any Lands in the Counties of New Castle, Kent or Sussex in Delaware*, 144; letter to Philadelphia Yearly Meeting on defense, 154-156; "Of the State of the British Plantations in America," :64-166; *Experimenta et meletemata de plantarum generatione*, 199-202, 204, 205; communications to Royal Society, 201, 203-205; on optics, 204-205; on Euclid, 206; on Pythagoras, 206; translation of "Distichs of Cato," 207, 212; translation of Cicero on old age, 207-208, 212; "The Duties of Man Deduced from Nature," 208-210

OPINIONS, on pacifism, 13-14, 28, 35, 39, 49-50, 154-156, 157; on danger of French aggression, 35-36, 107-108, 110, 163-165, 184; on government, 55, 72-73, 127, 155; on powers of Council, 72, 118, 127, 134, 140; on love of country, 99; on paper money, 124-125, 126, 148; on causes of poverty, 125, 128; on immigration, 159-160; on need for colonial union, 165; on Light Within, 210

PERSONAL CHARACTERISTICS, loyalty to Penn family, 30, 87, 113, 137-138; melancholy, 38, 40, 78, 166; satirized, 139, 148; appearance, 194-195

Logan, James, Jr., 191, 193
Logan, Patrick, JL's father, 6, 7, 8, 10
Logan, Sarah, JL's daughter, 94, 191
Logan, Sarah Read, JL's wife, 93-94, 111-112, 191
Logan, William, JL's brother, 7, 147, 190, 200
Logan, William, JL's son, 94, 154, 157-158, 190, 193
Loganian Library, 193-194
Logstown, treaty of (1748), 185
London, JL in, 81-87, 129-132
London Hope, ship, 128
Londonderry, siege of, 9, 107
Louisiana, 107, 163
Lower, Thomas, 58, 61, 64, 70, 73

Lower Counties, 4, 16, 21, 46, 51, 52-53, 114, 116-117, 124, 132, 143, 144, 157
Lurgan, Ireland, 7, 9, 10

MACHIN, JOHN, 203
"Magic squares," 211
Maize. See Corn, Indian
Malebranche, Nicolas de, 209
Markham, William, Deputy Governor, 16
Martin, Josiah, 84, 95, 96, 129, 191, 203, 210
Mary Hope, ship, 87
Maryland, 183; boundary dispute with, 115-117, 121-123, 124, 130-131, 170-178, 195
Mason and Dixon's line, 195
Mathematics, JL's knowledge of, 10, 78, 192, 205-206
Meade, William, 58, 61, 64, 70, 73
Mississippi Valley, 107, 184-185
Modest Enquiry into the Nature and Necessity of a Paper Currency, A, 148
Mompesson, Roger, 43, 58
"Moon illusion," 204
Moore, John, 31, 34, 39, 40, 70
More, Nicholas, Chief Justice of Pennsylvania, 68
More Just Vindication of the Honourable Sir William Keith, A, 144
Morris, Anthony, 56

NAVIGATION ACTS, 32
New Castle, Delaware, 32, 46, 47, 75, 170
New York, 97, 98, 105
Newton, Sir Isaac, 78, 98, 130, 192-193, 202, 205
Nicholson, Francis, Governor of Virginia, 37
Norris, Isaac, 18, 22, 42, 57-58, 59, 60, 70, 75, 79, 84, 86, 90, 119, 121, 122, 124-125, 131, 132, 187, 207

Norris, Isaac, Jr., 153
Nottingham lots, 115, 122, 170
Numismatics, 204
Nutimus, 178-179, 180, 181-183

OATHS. See Affirmation question
Observator's Trip to America, The, 139
"Of the State of the British Plantations in America," 164
Ogle, Samuel, Governor of Maryland, 170, 173, 174
Ohio Valley, 163, 168, 184
Optics, JL's interest in, 204-205
Owen, Dr. Griffith, 17, 22, 26

PACIFISM, QUAKER, 21, 35, 86, 153; JL's attitude toward, 13-14, 28, 35, 39, 49-50, 154-156, 157
Palatines. See German immigrants
Paper money, 120, 124-126, 132, 147-148
Paterson, James, 89
Pemberton, Israel, 93, 190-191, 212
Pemberton, Israel, Jr., 153
Penn, Hannah Callowhill, 12, 15, 18, 19, 85, 91-92, 113, 114, 123, 130, 143, 146; instructions to Governor Keith, 131-135
Penn, John, 18, 82, 137, 138, 142, 145, 146, 150, 159
Penn, Letitia, 12
Penn, Richard, 146
Penn, Springett, 114, 122
Penn, Thomas, 146, 167-170, 175, 180, 181
Penn, William, 11-14, 23, 26-27, 31, 34, 40, 53-54, 57-59, 64, 87, 116, 117, 155, 165; in America, 15-23; relations with Indians, 22, 101, 162, 178; proposes monopoly of fur trade, 25; loses Pennsylvania to Ford family, 28-29; negotiates for surrender of government to Crown, 38-39, 91, 114; in debtors' prison, 48, 70; grants Charter of Privileges, 51, 134,

136; ill health, 82, 91-92; writes "expostulatory letter" to Pennsylvania Friends, 83; death of, 113

Penn, William, Jr., 40, 41-43, 56-57, 82, 114

Pennsbury, 18-19, 22-23, 42, 178, 187

Perth Amboy, New Jersey, 36, 37, 97

Peters, Richard, 183

Philadelphia, Pennsylvania, 16, 144, 212, 214

Philadelphia, ship, 47

Philadelphia Monthly Meeting of Friends, 28, 77, 139

Philadelphia Yearly Meeting of Friends, 60; JL's letter to, on defense, 154

Philosophical Transactions of the Royal Society, 201, 203, 204, 205

Philosophy, JL's interest in, 192, 208-211

Plain Truth, 157

Portugal, trade with, 30, 79, 92; JL in, 80-81

Poulett, John, Earl, 114

Powder-tax episode, 46-47, 70

Preston, Samuel, 75

Ptolemy, 96, 204

Pythagoras, 206

QUADRANT, MARINER'S, 202-204

Quakerism, 3, 6, 198, 209, 210

Quary, Colonel Robert, 32, 33-34, 36-37, 38, 40, 41, 52, 53, 117

Queen Anne's War, 24, 48, 82, 168

Quitrents, 24, 25, 26, 27, 60, 87; defined, 20

Rachel, ship, 188

Randolph, Edward, 33

Rawle, Francis, 119, 120, 125

Reading, Reverend William, 129, 191

"Remonstrance" of 1704, 57-58, 73

Royal Society, 129-130, 200, 203; JL's communications to, 201, 203-205

Rutter, Thomas, 161, 162

Ryswick, Treaty of, 11

SACHEVERELL, HENRY, 81, 166

Sarah, ship, 188

Sassoonan, 106, 161-162, 169

Saur, Christopher, 156

Scotch-Irish immigrants, 106-107, 159, 161

Seneca Indians, 104

Sexual theory of plant generation, 199-202, 204

Seymour, John, Governor of Maryland, 44

Shawnee Indians, 104, 161, 163, 165, 168, 169-170, 185

Shickellamy, 163, 168

Shippen, Anne, 76-77

Shippen, Edward, 17, 22, 26, 38, 59, 60, 65, 76

Shippen, Edward, Jr., 188

Six Nations. *See* Iroquois Confederacy

"Slate-roof house," 17, 26

Sloane, Sir Hans, 129, 130, 204, 210

Smith, Captain Christopher, 104

Smith, Captain John, 116, 130

Smith, John, JL's son-in-law, 157, 195

Smith, Samuel, High Sheriff of Lancaster County, 173, 174, 176

Some Remedies Proposed for Restoring the Sunk Credit of the Province of Pennsylvania, 120

Spain in North America, 103

Spotswood, Alexander, Governor of Virgina, 103, 104, 105, 108, 110-111, 112, 143

Steel, James, 92, 167

Stenton, JL's country seat, 175, 181, 191, 194, 204; described, 186-187

Stenton, Scotland, 6

Story, Thomas, 18, 22, 26, 77, 149, 210

Strettell, Robert, 156

Susquehanna country, 121, 160-161, 169, 171-178
Sutherland, Earl of, 114

THOMAS, GABRIEL, 16
Thomas, George, Deputy Governor, 153, 157, 182, 183
Tishecunk, 178
Tories, English, 81, 82
Triumvirate of Pennsylvania, The, 148-149
Tulpehocken, Pennsylvania, 161, 162, 167, 169
Tuscarora War, 89

UTRECHT, TREATY OF, 100, 103, 118-119

VETCH, COLONEL SAMUEL, 49
Vice-Admiralty Courts. See Admiralty Courts

Vindication of the Legislative Power, A, 136-137, 138
Virginia, 104, 105, 108, 109, 163, 183
Virtuoso, character of the, 196-198, 204; JL as, Chapter XII

WALKING PURCHASE, 178-183
Walpole, Sir Robert, 163, 166
War of Jenkins's Ear, 153, 156
War of the Spanish Succession. See Queen Anne's War
Webb, Edward, 9, 11
Weiser, Conrad, 154, 156, 168, 174, 175, 179, 183, 184
West, Richard, 84
Whigs, English, 82, 166
Whitehead, George, 58, 64, 70, 73
Wilcox, Joseph, 56, 57, 72
Williamson, Joseph, 94, 129
Wollaston, William, 198, 199, 208
Wyandotte Indians, 185

YORK, DUKE OF. See James II